Llewellyn's

Witches' Datebook

2006

Featuring

Art by Jennifer Hewitson
Text by Elizabeth Barrette, Dallas Jennifer Cobb,
Ellen Dugan, Raven Grimassi, James Kambos,
Edain McCoy, Danny Pharr, K. D. Spitzer,
and Abby Willowroot

ISBN 0-7387-0154-8

2006

	JANUARY							FEBRUARY							MARCH							APRIL					
S	M	T	W	T	F	S	S	M	T	W	T	F	S	S	M	T	W	T	F	S	S	M	T	W	T	F	S
1	2	3	4	5	6	7				1	2	3	4				1	2	3	4							1
8	9	10	11	12	13	14	5	6	7	8	9	10	11	5	6	7	8	9	10	11	2	3	4	5	6	7	8
15	16	17	18	19	20	21	12	13	14	15	16	17	18	12	13	14	15	16	17	18	9	10	11	12	13	14	15
22	23	24	25	26	27	28	19	20	21	22	23	24	25	19	20	21	22	23	24	25	16	17	18	19	20	21	22
29	30	31					26	27	28					26	27	28	29	30	31		23	24	25	26	27	28	29
																					30						

	MAY							JUNE							JULY							AUGUST					
S	M	T	W	T	F	S	S	M	T	W	T	F	S	S	M	T	W	T	F	S	S	M	T	W	T	F	S
	1	2	3	4	5	6					1	2	3							1			1	2	3	4	5
7	8	9	10	11	12	13	4	5	6	7	8	9	10	2	3	4	5	6	7	8	6	7	8	9	10	11	12
14	15	16	17	18	19	20	11	12	13	14	15	16	17	9	10	11	12	13	14	15	13	14	15	16	17	18	19
21	22	23	24	25	26	27	18	19	20	21	22	23	24	16	17	18	19	20	21	22	20	21	22	23	24	25	26
28	29	30	31				25	26	27	28	29	30		23	24	25	26	27	28	29	27	28	29	30	31		
														30	31												

	SEPTEMBER							OCTOBER							NOVEMBER							DECEMBER					
S	M	T	W	T	F	S	S	M	T	W	T	F	S	S	M	T	W	T	F	S	S	M	T	W	T	F	S
					1	2	1	2	3	4	5	6	7				1	2	3	4						1	2
3	4	5	6	7	8	9	8	9	10	11	12	13	14	5	6	7	8	9	10	11	3	4	5	6	7	8	9
10	11	12	13	14	15	16	15	16	17	18	19	20	21	12	13	14	15	16	17	18	10	11	12	13	14	15	16
17	18	19	20	21	22	23	22	23	24	25	26	27	28	19	20	21	22	23	24	25	17	18	19	20	21	22	23
24	25	26	27	28	29	30	29	30	31					26	27	28	29	30			24	25	26	27	28	29	30
																					31						

2007

	JANUARY							FEBRUARY							MARCH							APRIL					
S	M	T	W	T	F	S	S	M	T	W	T	F	S	S	M	T	W	T	F	S	S	M	T	W	T	F	S
	1	2	3	4	5	6					1	2	3					1	2	3	1	2	3	4	5	6	7
7	8	9	10	11	12	13	4	5	6	7	8	9	10	4	5	6	7	8	9	10	8	9	10	11	12	13	14
14	15	16	17	18	19	20	11	12	13	14	15	16	17	11	12	13	14	15	16	17	15	16	17	18	19	20	21
21	22	23	24	25	26	27	18	19	20	21	22	23	24	18	19	20	21	22	23	24	22	23	24	25	26	27	28
28	29	30	31				25	26	27	28				25	26	27	28	29	30	31	29	30					

	MAY							JUNE							JULY							AUGUST					
S	M	T	W	T	F	S	S	M	T	W	T	F	S	S	M	T	W	T	F	S	S	M	T	W	T	F	S
		1	2	3	4	5						1	2	1	2	3	4	5	6	7				1	2	3	4
6	7	8	9	10	11	12	3	4	5	6	7	8	9	8	9	10	11	12	13	14	5	6	7	8	9	10	11
13	14	15	16	17	18	19	10	11	12	13	14	15	16	15	16	17	18	19	20	21	12	13	14	15	16	17	18
20	21	22	23	24	25	26	17	18	19	20	21	22	23	22	23	24	25	26	27	28	19	20	21	22	23	24	25
27	28	29	30	31			24	25	26	27	28	29	30	29	30	31					26	27	28	29	30	31	

	SEPTEMBER							OCTOBER							NOVEMBER							DECEMBER					
S	M	T	W	T	F	S	S	M	T	W	T	F	S	S	M	T	W	T	F	S	S	M	T	W	T	F	S
						1		1	2	3	4	5	6					1	2	3							1
2	3	4	5	6	7	8	7	8	9	10	11	12	13	4	5	6	7	8	9	10	2	3	4	5	6	7	8
9	10	11	12	13	14	15	14	15	16	17	18	19	20	11	12	13	14	15	16	17	9	10	11	12	13	14	15
16	17	18	19	20	21	22	21	22	23	24	25	26	27	18	19	20	21	22	23	24	16	17	18	19	20	21	22
23	24	25	26	27	28	29	28	29	30	31				25	26	27	28	29	30		23	24	25	26	27	28	29
30																					30	31					

Editing/design by K. M. Brielmaier

Cover illustration and interior art © 2005 by Jennifer Hewitson

Art on chapter openings © 2005 by Jennifer Hewitson

Cover design by Anne Marie Garrison

Art direction by Lynne Menturweck

Table of Contents

How to Use Llewellyn's *Witches' Datebook* 4
Walking the Path *by Raven Grimassi* 6
The Magic of Time *by Abby Willowroot* 10
Midnight Weeding *by Dallas Jennifer Cobb* 14
Personal Power *by Danny Pharr* 19
Forgotten Days of Power *by James Kambos* 24
January 28
February 38
March 46
April 55
May 64
June 72
July 81
August 90
September 98
October 107
November 116
December 124
About the Authors 134
Appendix 136
Addresses 140

How to Use Llewellyn's *Witches' Datebook*

Welcome to Llewellyn's *Witches' Datebook 2006!* This datebook was designed especially for Witches, Pagans, and magical people. Use it to plan sabbat celebrations, magic, Full Moon rites, and even dentist and doctor appointments! Below is a symbol key to some of the features of this datebook.

MOON QUARTERS: The Moon's cycle is divided into four quarters, which are noted in the calendar pages along with their exact times. When the Moon changes quarter, both quarters are listed, as well as the time of the change. In addition, a symbol for the new quarter is placed where the numeral for the date usually appears.

MOON IN THE SIGNS: Approximately every two-and-a-half days the Moon moves from one zodiac sign to the next. The sign that the Moon is in at the beginning of the day (midnight Eastern Standard Time) is noted next to the quarter listing. If the Moon changes signs that day, there will be a notation saying "☽ enters" followed by the symbol for the sign it is entering.

MOON VOID-OF-COURSE: Just before the Moon enters a new sign it will make one final aspect (angular relationship) to another planet. Between that last aspect and the entrance of the Moon into the next sign it is said to be void-of-course. Activities begun when the Moon is void rarely come to fruition, or they turn out very differently than planned.

PLANETARY MOVEMENT: When a planet or asteroid moves from one sign into another, this change (called an *ingress*) is noted on the calendar pages with the exact time. The Moon and Sun are considered planets in this case. The planets (except for the Sun and Moon) can also appear to move backward as seen from the Earth. This is called a *planetary retrograde*, and is noted on the calendar pages with the symbol ℞. When the planet begins to move forward, or direct, again, it is marked D, and the time is also noted.

PLANTING AND HARVESTING DAYS: The best days for planting and harvesting are noted on the calendar pages with a seedling icon (planting) and a basket icon (harvesting).

TIME ZONE CHANGES: The times and dates of all astrological phenomena in this datebook are based on Eastern time. If you live outside of the Eastern time zone, you will need to make the following changes: Pacific Time subtract three hours; Mountain Time subtract two hours; Central Time subtract one hour; and Alaska/Hawaii subtract five hours. All data is adjusted for Daylight Saving Time.

Planets

☉	Sun	
☽	Moon	
☿	Mercury	
♀	Venus	
♂	Mars	
♃	Jupiter	
♄	Saturn	
♅	Uranus	
♆	Neptune	
♇	Pluto	
⚷	Chiron	
⚳	Ceres	
⚴	Pallas	
⚵	Juno	
⚶	Vesta	

Signs

♈	Aries	
♉	Taurus	
♊	Gemini	
♋	Cancer	
♌	Leo	
♍	Virgo	
♎	Libra	
♏	Scorpio	
♐	Sagittarius	
♑	Capricorn	
♒	Aquarius	
♓	Pisces	

Motion

℞ Retrograde
D Direct

1st Quarter/New Moon ☽
2nd Quarter ☽

3rd Quarter/Full Moon ☺
4th Quarter ☽

☽ **Tuesday** ◄——— Day and date
1st Libra ◄——— Moon's quarter and sign
2nd Quarter 4:01 am ◄——— Moon quarter change
☽ v/c 4:01 am ◄——— Moon void-of-course
☽ enters ♏ 9:30 am ◄——— Moon sign change/ingress
♄ ℞ 10:14 am ◄——— Planetary retrograde
Color: Gray ◄——— Color of the day

Planting day ——➤ 🌱

Harvesting day ——➤ 🧺

5

Walking the Path
by Raven Grimassi

In the busy and often stressful life of modern times, it is a real challenge to maintain a daily spiritual perspective. Advertisements, road signs, commercials, news, and other distractions almost constantly bombard us. Many of us sit in congested traffic each day as we travel to and from work. The weekend arrives; we deal with chores and try to find a little recreational time with friends and family. Can we really live a satisfying spiritual life amidst all of these challenges?

Witchcraft, as a spiritual tradition, is focused upon a set of personal codes and personal honor. What makes a person a Witch is how he or she views life and his or her place in the scheme of things. Being a Witch is more about who you are than about what you do.

Being fully present in the moment is an important and vital aspect of consciousness for the Witch. Yesterday is only a memory, and tomorrow is just the promise of something yet to come. The only reality in which we exist is the present moment. We cannot change the past nor operate in the future, but we can fully participate in the present.

When I was a young child, I played in the backyard while my mother worked in her herb garden. She would call me to her side and ask, "Did I ever tell you what we do with this herb?" If I showed any signs of being distracted or inattentive, my mother would smile and say, "Well, some other time." No amount of pleading would change her mind, for the moment had come and gone. She wasted no time on those who failed to be present in the moment. In my mother's garden I learned the importance of being present and attentive to the opportunities around me.

Spiritual moments often arise in the least-expected ways and under the most mundane of circumstances. I recall one experience that involved being picked up by a driver I had hired to take me to the airport one early morning. I'm definitely not a morning person, and without a cup or two of coffee I tend to avoid conversation.

The morning the driver arrived I was running late and had not had any coffee. The driver was quite elderly and frail, and so I loaded all the bags and got into the front seat. My traveling companion sat in the back seat. As we drove to the airport, the driver initiated a conversation. I could sense my companion chuckling because she knew that for me this event required coffee.

As we drove, he talked about his life in the military as a newly married young man. War had taken him overseas, and he left his wife alone in a housing development. Her nearest relative was two thousand miles away. He spoke to me of kindnesses shown to his wife by strangers during his absence. The driver spoke of his first home, raising his children, jobs he'd held, and his feelings about retirement.

As we drove I listened to the old man's story. During the forty-five minute drive he shared his happiness, his regrets, and his broken and realized dreams. When he dropped me off at the airport and drove away, I realized that this had been a significant spiritual moment. How easy it would have been to have half-listened and pretended interest. But instead I welcomed an embrace by a gentle soul who shared his story with a total stranger. He offered me the gift of his life's experience. I wonder how often we reject such gifts because we choose not to be fully present in the moment.

The circumstances of our lives can often cause us to be exclusively self-focused. Modern life frequently pushes time demands to extreme limits. We often find ourselves rushing off to what we need to do rather than being fully in the moment in which we find ourselves. This can place a lot of stress on us and upon those with whom we share a relationship. Add the agenda of people who don't like us, and life can present significant challenges to maintaining a spiritual heart and mind.

7

One of the greatest challenges a Witch must face is perseverance. We must walk the path we have chosen despite its burdens and pitfalls. A Witch holds true to his or her spirituality despite how others treat him or her. For the Witch there can be no situational ethics. The personal code must apply regardless of the temptations and self-justifications that may present themselves. The Witch does not modify his or her integrity to suit the situation or the relationship at hand.

In witchcraft we draw from nature and learn from her as well. The seasons teach us that everything operates in cycles. Seasons of gain give way to seasons of decline, and nothing remains in one phase or the other. Each season has its gifts and its challenges. Through this we grow and mature as spiritual beings. It is pointless to rage against winter or cling to summer.

In the spring a tree begins to bud, and in summer it flowers. In fall its leaves begin to wither, and in winter its branches are bare. But the tree does not love one season and hate another. A tree is always in tune with its environment, and in each season it is simply a tree in spring, summer, fall, or winter. For the Witch this alignment is the same, and he or she merges and harmonizes with the environment that prevails.

At the core of the Witch's spirituality is the understanding that all things are connected and interwoven. Divinity dwells within us as the divine spark, just as our souls dwell within physical bodies. The divine spark is the meeting place between us and divinity, between us and the world in which we live. All living things share that same spark of divinity. The next time you're hurrying down a street or rushing in traffic, take a look at the plants, animals, and creatures around you. Notice that you're the only living thing that is trying to be in a time that awaits you rather than where you are already.

It is often this detachment from the moment, and from the world we share with other beings, that causes us to lose our spiritual focus. The next time you're on your way to somewhere else, touch a leaf on a tree as you walk down the street. Look briefly out your car window and note the joy of a bird upon the wind. In all that you must do each day, be part of what is taking place around you. Be aware that you are part of the world in which you live, and that you share the divine gift of life with all the beings on this planet.

Earlier I referred to the lessons nature can teach us, and to the seasons of a tree. Our ancient ancestors venerated trees for a variety of reasons. One of those reasons is because the tree can teach us much through observation. What is it that a tree can tell us about life and spirituality?

Trees teach us about rootedness, position, and strength. The roots of a tree remind us that much goes unseen by our eyes, and that we must look beneath the surface. The tree reminds us that the roots provide the nourishment that sustains life. Roots provide foundation and the strength to hold fast against adversity.

Branches teach us about the importance of youth and maturity. Fruit grows only on the old wood of the branch, and its seeds ensure future generations. The new branches quickly produce flowers and attract the process of fertilization and renewal. Together the old and new branches contribute equally to the future of the tree and the future of the grove.

The spirit of the tree teaches us to serve others as we serve ourselves. While the tree stands and proclaims its place in the world, it also provides shade, shelter, home, and food for other beings. From its center it teaches us the lessons of its spirit:

- Have a foundation with deep roots, and stand firm in your place within the world.

- Reach upward to touch lofty things, and outward to extend yourself to the world.

- Provide shade for those who need rest, and shelter for those who come to you.

- Bear fruit, and be abundant.

- In the winters of your life, conserve your resources. In your springs, take advantage of the opportunities for new growth. In your summers, expand, thrive, and reach new heights. In your falls, release what no longer serves, make preparations, and await renewal.

- When all is said and done, leave behind some seeds.

The Magic of Time

by Abby Willowroot

Time is a great mystery, hidden within the ordinary. From the earliest human experiences, time has been a focal point of our thought and actions. Time is the mystery of things becoming and unbecoming. Shaman and mystics leap into the unknown streams of alternative time and bring back visions, prophecies, and secrets. It is within these realms of altered time that all mystical experiences occur.

Stonehenge, Chaco Canyon, the pyramids at Giza, Mystery Hill, Mayan pyramids, and ancient structures all over the world mark important times of the year for the people who built them. We are just beginning to understand how amazingly sophisticated these structures are in computing the passage of time. Our calendars today measure our time just as the ancients measured their time. The Chinese, the Hopi, the Maya, the Aztec, western society, and others all have calendars measuring time and relating it to significant events, past and future. Some of the world's calendars are based on the Sun and some are based on the Moon.

We all slip into the "stream of time" at our birth, and flow along within it for the rest of our lives. Our individual journeys are as unique as the ways we interact with time throughout our lives. Astrology is based on the exact time and place we enter the stream of time. Each point in the flow of time has its own properties, characteristics, challenges, and gifts.

Transcending time has always been the great dream of humanity. Ancient people called upon shaman, priestess, and priest to guide them through the mysteries of alternative time. Hindus and Buddhists speak of escaping the wheel of time's endless cycle of reincarnations. Christians, Jews, and Muslims speak of eternity, and many tribal religions speak of the ancestors and the time before. At the center of all religious and mystical experience is time.

Our thoughts and speech are filled with words relating to time. We speak of then, now, soon, when, later, tomorrow, today, yesterday, future, past, and never. We often talk about "a long time ago" or "sometime in the future," and about good times or bad times, running out of time and having enough time. There is no denying the human connection with matters of time.

We measure time by moments, seconds, minutes, hours, days, weeks, months, years, decades, centuries, millennia, eternity. With the passage of each, we sort, analyze, discard, or save. Our holidays are all celebrations of a certain point in time. They mark our births or someone else's, or the moment something great occurred. History, archeology, physics, geology, cosmology, and astrology are all deeply concerned with time. It is as if our own internal clocks drive us to anchor time in the world around us in some concrete way. It is this need that drives our human obsession with time. Our connection with time is at the foundation of all we call sacred and magic.

Dusk and dawn are times of the day often referred to as being "between time." Many believe the fabric of ordinary time is stretched thin at these brief transition points between day and night. These are the hours that stir a sense of the eternal and timeless in all of us. It is as if we sense the coming and going of the Sun from our space and time prompts us to take some sort of sacred action. These mystical hours signal us to stop and experience our own eternal selves, the selves that live beyond the bounds of time. A sunrise touched our ancient ancestors as powerfully and profoundly as it touches us. The vibrant dimming or growing of the light as the Sun merges with the horizon inspires transcendent feelings. At these times, we most easily sense our own powers to move between ordinary and mystical time.

11

The Metaphysics of Time

Thousands of years ago the ancient Hindus looked deep into time and formed beliefs. The accuracy of some of these insights are being reaffirmed by modern physicists and cosmologists. "Deep field" pictures from the Hubble telescope have thrown scientists into a quandary about what modern science believed was true about time. These deep-space pictures defy quantum physics' view of time. Now many leading scientists say time travel could be possible, and there is much speculation about parallel universes, eleven dimensions, and the multiverse.

Metaphysics and physics are dancing together, mingling ideas about time and space from both new theories and ancient beliefs. Unique theories of time have come from Plato, Socrates, Copernicus, Aristotle, Nostradamus, Einstein, Hawking, Gödel, Kozyrev, Steinhardt, Turok, Lynds, and many others. Science is magic, and magic is science; in today's reality they are not very far apart, and yesterday's science fiction is becoming today's science fact.

Today, magical rituals and celebrations are held after creating a symbolic sacred space. This ritual space is considered to be outside the stream of ordinary time and space. We all understand instinctively that time is powerful, mystical, and can be transformed, yet few of us consciously practice working with alternative modes of time.

Can you work with time and alter it in your own life? You already do, although you may not be aware of it. We know that time can be manipulated and stretched, compressed, lengthened and shortened—or at least our perception of it can be.

When you are excited, changes happen that affect time. Your heart races, your metabolism speeds up, colors brighten, sounds amplify, everything comes into clearer focus, and time slows down. That is because your perception of time is stretching and your brain has a chance to really notice these things.

When you are resting or sleeping, your metabolism slows down and time seems to speed up, passing more quickly. When we age, our metabolism slows down, and this is why the older we get the faster time seems to go. Young people experience faster time too; sometimes the hours of play speed by and you can't really account for how you spent them. This is not a fantasy; this is a fact of how time interacts with our minds and bodies. You feel there is less time, and you are right—there *is* less time.

Metaphysical time works in similar ways. A shaman or yogi can go into a trance state that alters his metabolism, speeding or slowing his experience of time, while people around him are still living in "ordinary time." Some claim that in a trance state they can slow time to the point where it moves backwards into the past, or speed it forward into the future. Others claim to be able to step into the stream of time at any point they desire.

Temporal Experiments

Experiment with time for yourself. Put paper, pen, and a clock on the floor. Sit down quietly and relax, slowing your breathing. Look at the clock and mark the time down on paper. Put the clock behind you and don't look at it again till you think ten minutes have passed. Draw doodles, write your thoughts, or just sit there. Don't get excited or anxious, just be. When you think it has been ten minutes, look at the clock and mark down the time,

A few minutes later, exercise, run, dance, do whatever "revs you up." Think about things that interest you a lot. Sit down, but this time keep yourself revved up and don't take time to relax. Mark the time down, immediately begin to doodle, draw, or write, but stay excited. When you think ten minutes have passed, look at the clock again and mark down the time.

Compare the times. How close did you come to ten minutes? Is there a difference in the amount of time you spent doing the experiments? Are you surprised by the results? If this is your first conscious exercise in working with time shifting, it may take a few tries to understand. Try again in a few days. Soon, with practice, you will be able to adjust your perception of time with your mind.

Mastering this simple skill will allow you to swim freely in the stream of time, changing it as needed. The magic of time is a journey worth exploring.

Midnight Weeding
by Dallas Jennifer Cobb

The dark phase of the Moon brings powerful energy to magical work. Not only mere diminishing spells but utter banishing can be done during the complete dark of the Moon. Whether for weeds in the garden, bad habits, or situations in your life, the Dark Moon can help you get rid of things unwanted.

Do not confuse Dark Moon magic with the dark arts, or black magic. This article is not about harmful spell work or bad intent, but about the Dark Moon, the Dark Goddess, and banishing spells. With a focus on magical gardening, this article will be of particular interest to gardeners and herbalists, and those who see the garden as a metaphor for life itself.

Magical gardening, midnight weeding, and Dark Moon magic are intended to be tools used to root out things in your own garden or life, and not things in other people's lives. What may be an obnoxious weed to one person is a healing herb to another.

Magical gardeners tend only to their own plot.

The Cycles of the Moon

In everything there is a balance between light and dark. During the lunar cycle of twenty-nine-and-a-half days, the Moon is born, lives, dies, and then is reborn. For banishing magic, we are interested in the "dead" or completely dark phase of the Moon.

Born as the New Moon, it sprouts like a seed under the Earth, not visible until it grows above the Earth. Called the Crescent Moon, a thin sliver of moonlight is visible in the western sky in the late afternoon and early evening. Waxing into life, the Moon grows in size to be First Quarter Moon, visible from noon to midnight. The Gibbous Moon rises before sunset, and the Full Moon rises just as the Sun sets, her beauty luminous in the sky through much of the night. Magic done during the waxing phase of the Moon increases energy and promotes new growth.

During the latter part of life, the Moon wanes. The Disseminating Moon rises after sunset, one hour later each night. The Last Quarter Moon rises at midnight and sets at noon. The Balsamic Moon represents the turning under. It rises at 3:00 am and sets mid-afternoon. It is the last sliver of Moon seen in the eastern sky in the very early morning. The Balsamic Moon is a time for dreams and visions, for being in touch with your intuitive self. Spiritual understanding is closer as the Moon prepares for the descent to the underworld. Use the energy of the waning Moon to aid magic meant to decrease or diminish energy.

The old Moon wanes; like composting matter, it breaks down and provides nutrients to the soil of life. The Dark Moon seems barren—without illumination or enlightenment. It is a time for magic work on things we want gone. Finished. Ended. Dead.

The Dark Moon

The period of time between ten-and-a-half and fourteen days after the Full Moon is often called the New Moon. The Moon and Sun are in conjunction, so they rise and set together. Sunlight overpowers the nearby Moon during the day and the Moon is on the other side of the Earth, with the Sun, at night, and not visible in the sky at all during this phase, except during a solar eclipse.

While astrologers refer to this as the New Moon, I consider it a misnomer. For the purpose of this article I will call the days when no moonlight is visible the Dark Moon, and New Moon will refer to the early waxing phase of the Moon, when a thin sliver of light is visible.

When the old Moon ceases to be seen, it is has symbolically died. But the lunar cycle does not stop; it is reformed, reorganized, and later reborn as the New Moon. Our lives can be reformed and reorganized during the Dark Moon phase. It is a time for removing unwanted energies, culling the weeds in our life, and replenishing our inner soil.

While this period is three-and-a-half days long, for the purpose of Dark Moon magic the most powerful time is the one day right in the middle of the darkness, when the Moon is fully inhabiting the underworld. The time just before is powerful for doing diminishing spells, but since there is still a fraction of light in that darkness, it is a diminishing energy and not a banishing energy. And the third day of the Dark Moon period is not to be used for diminishing or banishing spells, because although the Moon is not visible to the eye, it is now waxing, growing in energy and size. Magical work done at this time promotes growth.

The Dark Goddess

The Dark Moon is often personified by the Dark Goddess, ruler of winter and the underworld. The Dark Goddess is both destroyer and renewer, the wise Crone who will die that a child may be born, an old soul reincarnated.

Known as Kali, Morrigan, Cailleach, Lilith, and Hecate, the Dark Goddess rules over the night, crossroads, life and death, magical arts, secret knowledge, and oracles. Animals of the night and those that live below the Earth's surface are her familiars.

The Dark Goddess brings transformation, bidding us look back over time so that we learn from our mistakes. Knowing what habits, people, and things to banish from our lives helps us to focus our spiritual energy for the cycle to come.

When doing Dark Moon magic, invoke the Dark Goddess in one of her forms. She will assist with waning energy spells and banishing spells, and in reincarnation. She will help you refocus and regenerate, bringing justice to bear and goodness to light.

Dark Moon Magic

The Dark Moon is the time for working magic with things that need to be finished, banished, or let go: addictions, fear, divorce, enemies, injustice, obstacles, separation, and stopping stalkers and thieves. It is also a time for ridding oneself of bad habits and binding spells, for exploring our dark selves, and for understanding our angers and passions.

For magical weeding, and work with anything that responds strongly to light, it is recommended that you do the magical work in complete darkness—either in a completely darkened room or at night on the twelfth to thirteenth day after the Full Moon. On a physical level, farmers and gardeners have long known the effect of the light of the Moon on plants. On a symbolic level, light represents knowl-
edge, wisdom, understanding, and enlightenment. If you are trying to banish obnoxious weeds or a destructive habit, it is better to work in complete darkness. Habits and weeds, like all living things, will struggle to survive.

Whether you are physically or symbolically working to banish something, it is better to give no warning of your actions. Arrive under the cover of darkness, work swiftly and with great focus, and uproot what is unwanted from the soil of your garden, or your life.

Midnight Weeding

Effective weed banishing is best done while the Moon is dark. If you cannot do it then, do it on the late nights of the Balsamic Moon, as the energy of the Moon is waning. If the Moon has started to wax, but is not visible, the energy is still one of waxing, and will therefore stimulate growth and resurrection of the weeds.

Since you are weeding at night during the Dark Moon, you must identify the weeds that you want to banish during the day, when you can see them and clearly identify them. Later, you can go to the garden in the darkness, using a candle or small flashlight to find your way, and quickly locate the weeds. Then, when you are ready to weed them out, shut off the light, meditate, and work your magic.

As you pull the weeds out, say:

> *You are no longer needed here,*
> *You are no longer wanted here,*
> *Compost your energy to aid and be near,*
> *But remove yourself from here.*

Give thanks for the weeds and the role they play in the garden. Thank them for all that they have done and will do, and encourage them to return their nutrients to the soil, and then place them in the compost.

For horribly invasive weeds, don't put them in your domestic compost pile, as they can sometimes sprout and grow. It is better to find a spot where such weeds would be welcomed and appreciated: along river banks or precipice edges, where weeds help stabilize soil and prevent erosion. In spots such as these they are free to be abundant, their pervasive energy suited to the task at hand.

If you are going to do this, pull the weeds in complete darkness and remove them from your garden. Store them in a bucket overnight, and take them to the new site once the Dark Moon has started to wax. This will energetically assist reestablishment in the new location.

Intuitive Gardening

The Dark Moon is also a time for doing intuitive gardening. Between death and rebirth is the void—the realm of long-buried memories and perceptions. During the Dark Moon, look into the void to find the truth that is hidden in the darkness. Explore what is hidden in the dark recesses of your mind, that which you are afraid to face, and through the cycle bring these things to the surface and into the light.

Intuitively weed out the harmful habits or situations in your life. Trusting intuition, let the Wise Mother speak to you and guide you as you garden. Intuitively reach for the weeds, remove them, and let the light shine more fully on the fertile and beautiful plants that grow in your magical garden.

Fertile be the magical garden.

Further Reading

Conway, D.J. *Moon Magick: Myth & Magic, Crafts & Recipes, Rituals & Spells*. St. Paul: Llewellyn, 1995.

McCoy, Edain. *Magick & Rituals of the Moon*. St. Paul: Llewellyn, 2001.

Morrison, Dorothy. *Everyday Moon Magic: Spells & Rituals for Abundant Living*. St. Paul: Llewellyn, 2004.

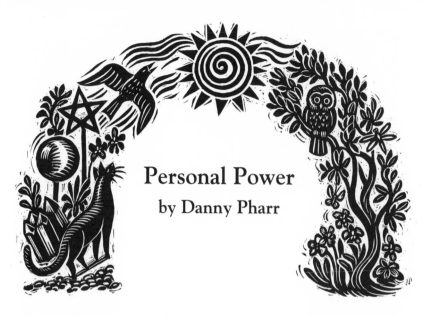

Personal Power
by Danny Pharr

Personal power is the key to success in ritual, at work, in relationships, and in life. Without personal power, success is nearly impossible. When you do not believe, at your core, in yourself, success will always be elusive. Personal power is believing in yourself.

Personal power might involve lightning shooting from your fingers, a whole room of people frozen in their tracks, or commanding an earthquake. More likely examples are truthfully saying how you feel, confidently asking your boss for a raise, saying "no" without reservation, saying "yes" with joy, and making immediate decisions that enhance your higher good. These are all manifestations of core power; they are the tree, which is supported by an unseen root. Core power, the root of all successes, is the most basic of beliefs, but it is so often diminished in our society. Core power is believing in yourself.

The reason magic works is because of belief, because of faith. When casting a spell, you must believe you can do so successfully or your effort is pointless. The same is true for driving a car, balancing your checkbook, or programming your VCR. If you believe you can, you will; if you believe you cannot, you will not. If you believe you might, you probably will not. To claim to own your personal power is to believe in yourself. The only person who can diminish your personal power and self-belief is you. No one can take that from you. But you can give it away.

Claiming personal power is about sealing your power leaks, about empowering yourself and promoting yourself, about respecting yourself and loving yourself. Claiming personal power is believing in yourself. In order to consistently embody belief in yourself, to turn up the volume on your core power, you must make use of the five power techniques: asking for what you want, speaking the truth, taking responsibility for your experience, paying attention, and keeping your agreements.

Asking for What You Want

In this society, when you want something, you are expected to nicely hint, gesture, or maneuver your way into getting it. When a package is heavy and you want someone to help, you make a half-hearted attempt at lifting it and emit an audible grunt. When you do not enjoy the taste of your meal at a restaurant, you do not send it back and order something else. You might say you weren't hungry, all the while secretly hoping that someone will offer to discount the bill.

You go through all of this rather than simply asking for help with a heavy load or saying you would like another entree. Asking for what you want is direct, powerful, and effective. Most people, upon hearing a direct request, will help you to achieve your request. We are a helpful people and we do not like to disappoint others. Ask for what you want and you will probably get it. Ask for what you want and you will believe in yourself.

Speaking the Truth

When a person lies, a part of that person dies. When you do not tell the truth about your thoughts, feelings, or actions, you are telling yourself that you are not worthy of the truth, that you are less than the other person, that you are only what others believe you to be. When you fear the judgment of others, you have given them the responsibility to judge you, the prerogative to decide what is right and wrong for you, and the freedom to shape you and your life at their whims.

Speaking the truth allows you to decide who you are and how your life will be shaped. Speaking the truth tells your subconscious that you are proud of yourself, that you will not let anyone hold sway over your thoughts and deeds. Speaking the truth is believing in yourself.

Taking Responsibility for Your Experience

Don't be a victim to anyone. In other words, do not make excuses—make choices. When you are late and excuse yourself due to traffic, or the babysitter, or an unusually long meeting, you are telling the other person, and yourself, that you were a victim to traffic, the babysitter, or a meeting, and that these excuses are your master. Taking responsibility doesn't mean accepting the blame, but it does mean accepting that you are the one who will fix the problem.

If it is important enough, you will do it. For example, arriving on time for work is your responsibility, and arriving late simply means you did not allot enough time, regardless of the excuse. If the boss wrote a check to you for one million dollars and said it was yours when you arrived on time for work every day for a month, the chances are you would find a way to be at work on time, at least for the next month, even if being at work on time meant sleeping there. Admitting what is most important in your life gives you power. Taking responsibility for your experience is believing in yourself.

Paying Attention

Multitasking is the bane of a spiritual existence. Eating dinner while sitting in front of the television is an example of how to not enjoy your food while not watching your television program. Paying attention is about living life in every moment. When you are not focused on your task, you are blindly walking through life, hoping for something better. But when you completely focus on your task at hand, regardless of what that task might be, you enter liminal space—that place where nothing else exists, where you become your activity. This is joy: becoming so engrossed that nothing else matters. To paraphrase Nietzsche: "Ultimate joy exists when you are living in such a manner that you would choose to repeat this life over and over, for eternity." Paying attention is the source of joy. Paying attention is believing in yourself.

Keeping Your Agreements

Just do it! Nike didn't choose the phrase, "Just try it!" for a reason. Because trying means failing. If you are only going to try, then you are leaving the back door open to failure. When you intend only to try, you

tell yourself before you start that you will not succeed, that you are not good enough to succeed, but that you need to make a showing because you are expected to do so. Either do it or do not. Trying is a loss of self-respect. Keeping your agreements is doing what you say you will do, with other people, and most importantly with yourself. When you do not keep your agreements, you are telling yourself that you cannot be trusted. When you do what you say you will, you are proud of your accomplishments, and begin to believe that nothing is beyond your grasp. Keeping your agreements is believing in yourself.

Keeping your power in your personal life means also keeping your power in your magical, work, and spiritual life. When you hide from who and what you are, when you downplay your beliefs, you are allowing others to shape your experience of life.

Stand up and be counted! When you have something to say, say it; when you emote, express it; when you want something, ask for it; when you want the truth, speak it; when you want an experience, do it; when you want love, give it. When you want other people to believe in you, believe in yourself.

Ritual of Personal Power

Cast a circle with candles representing the four elements. You will be making a bracelet and will need five beads, a small cord, and scissors. Take the bead representing elemental air in your hand, hold it to the east, and, as you slide the cord through the bead and tie a knot on either side of the bead, speak the first incantation. Repeat this process for each bead in each direction. While speaking the final binding phrase, comfortably tie the bracelet around your wrist and cut the ends to the desired length.

"I infuse this bead with the power of speaking my truth, energized by the element of air. As I tie these knots, I bind myself to this promise and this power.

"I infuse this bead with the power of keeping my agreements, energized by the element of fire. As I tie these knots, I bind myself to this promise and this power.

"I infuse this bead with the power of taking responsibility for my experience, energized by the element of water. As I tie these knots, I bind myself to this promise and this power.

"I infuse this bead with the power of asking for what I want, energized by the element of earth. As I tie these knots, I bind myself to this promise and this power.

"I infuse this bead with the power of paying attention, energized by spirit. As I tie these knots, I bind myself to this promise and this power.

"With this bracelet, power is mine, for now, when I need it, and for all time. I wear this bracelet, power divine, always outward, always inward, always I'll shine. This promise I make to the Goddess and to me, and as this is my word, so mote it be."

Further Reading

Cunningham, Scott. *Wicca: A Guide for the Solitary Practitioner.* St. Paul: Llewellyn, 1988.

Murphy-Hiscock, Arin. *Power Spellcraft for Life: The Art of Crafting & Casting for Positive Change.* Avon, Mass.: Adams, 2005.

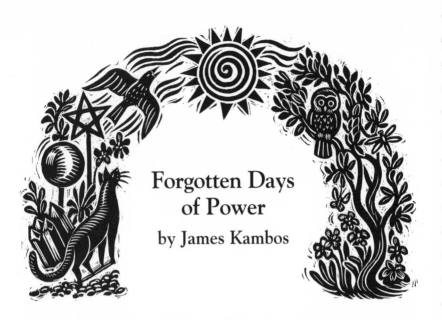

Forgotten Days of Power

by James Kambos

H olidays help us measure time. They serve to reassure us that the changing seasons will never end. I spent much of my childhood on a farm, and became aware of the rhythm of the seasons at an early age, so as an adult it was fitting that I wanted to learn about the nature-oriented Wiccan religion. I was especially fascinated with the eight major Wiccan holidays: Imbolc, Ostara, Beltane, Litha, Lughnasadh, Mabon, Samhain, and Yule. These holidays are frequently referred to as the "Eight Days of Power."

While researching the origins of these holidays, I discovered that, since ancient times, cultures and religions around the world have observed many other special days as well. In fact, many more. In most cases, these forgotten days of power are no longer observed, or have partly been absorbed into other religious, cultural, or national traditions.

What follows is a list of seven long-forgotten holidays. These are days that at one time were important milestones on the wheel of the year. The essence of some of these days is still with us, but many are now overshadowed by other major holidays. In other cases, changes in calendar systems have made modern societies forget these old festivals. Where possible, I've included spells or rituals to enhance the meaning of these days.

Keep in mind, these are only a few of the old holidays which were once celebrated. There are many more waiting to be rediscovered.

Other Days of Power

January 7: Return of the Sun

In northern Europe, this was believed to be the day that the power of the Sun began to return and animals stirred during their winter hibernation. To observe this day, toast the return of the Sun with grain- or fruit-based beverages (beer, ale, or cider would be good choices). Or stand before a fire during the morning and cast a prosperity spell. Finish your ritual by placing a wheat or cornhusk doll into the fire to help fuel the energy of the strengthening Sun.

February 13: St. Valentine's Eve

This day has been celebrated as a magical day since medieval times. It was believed that this was the day birds selected a mate and began to sing. I've noticed that on or about this day house finches fly about my yard in pairs, selecting a nesting site.

During the Victorian era, this day began to be referred to as St. Valentine's Eve and rivaled Valentine's Day itself in popularity. On this day, romantic foods were prepared and divinations of all kinds were done to determine who might be a future lover. Prophetic dreams to reveal a new romance were eagerly sought. One of the oldest but least-known ways to do this is to take three white candy-coated almonds and charge them with your magical intent. Without thinking of a specific person, place the almonds beneath your pillow at bedtime. Expect your dreams to give you a clue as to the identity of a future romantic partner.

March 21: The Creation of Time

Many occultists believe this was the day the Divine Power created the Sun, Moon, and stars—which would make this the day time began. If that isn't reason enough to honor this day, there are also other rituals taking place today which are quite noteworthy.

The Iranian New Year, *No Ruz*, is usually observed on this day and is rich with symbolism. People plant small dishes of wheat or lentil seeds; the sprouts represent the New Year and the arrival of spring. Tables are set with pastel-colored eggs, fruits, and pastries. You may wish to follow the Iranian custom and place a curving, gnarled branch or twig upon your altar, to symbolize that life itself has many twists and turns.

This would be a splendid day to review your own desires and goals. Have you stayed on the path you've chosen? If not, think about where you went off course and try again. Spend the day getting your emotional and spiritual house in order, so you can face the coming season of renewal with confidence.

April 25, and moveable dates in late spring: Rogation Days
The Major Rogation Day is April 25, and the Minor Rogation Days are the three days before the Christian observance of the Feast of the Ascension, which falls forty days after Easter. These days are a time for prayers asking for blessings of bounty and good crops.

Rogation is derived from the Latin word rogare, which means "to ask." This Christian observance parallels, and is probably derived from, the ancient Roman tradition of blessing the fields. Roman farmers would walk their fields asking the gods of agriculture to bestow a bountiful harvest. In colonial America, Rogation Sunday (the Sunday before Ascension Day) was the day farmers and clergy would walk the newly planted fields, praying for healthy crops.

Pagans may use this time to bless the home and garden. Since most of us no longer have fields to bless, we can call upon our favorite deity to ensure our homes are spiritually cleansed, or ask that a specific project be fruitful. If you garden, sprinkle the soil with water you have blessed. You could also perform a spell to protect and bless home, property, and career. After your ritual, make a donation to a food bank. Then purchase some flowers or early vegetables from a local farmer's market.

June 15: The Fires of Summer
Since ancient times, mid-June was an important point on the calendar, used to "guide" the Sun on its path, which eventually peaked at the Summer Solstice. In celebration, needfires were built, and as the flames climbed skyward, people chanted while raising their arms as a sign of gratitude. From these needfires, branches shaped into circular forms were lighted and rolled downhill.

These rites continued well into the twentieth century. In the Greek village where my mother lived as a child, she remembers this solar ritual. She recalls how the men of the village would ignite hoops from the needfire and then jump through them as a form of purification. The burning hoops naturally symbolized the Sun's healing rays.

To create your own solar rite, light a large orange candle on your altar. Surround it with four yellow votives. As you light the orange candle say, "Candle burn, let the Sun return." Light the votive candles, one for each season, and then say, "Candles burn, let the seasons turn." Gazing at the burning candles, think of the things in your life you wish to energize—love, friendships, or any other activity. Or you may use this ritual to purify magical tools.

August 13: Diana's Day

The ancient Romans set aside this day to honor their beloved deity, Diana. Great and powerful, Diana is a warrior goddess figure. She is the compassionate protector of the disadvantaged. As a Moon goddess, she is also identified with women, childbirth, hunters, animals, and all rural places. Healing and success fall under her powers as well.

Since trees are sacred to Diana, invoke her spirit in a wooded area. To do this, plan a picnic or cookout. Served grilled meats and fruits. After your feast, cast a spell for general well-being and success. Thank Diana for listening to you by leaving a small gift on a tree branch such as an ornament shaped like an animal, a crescent Moon, or a star.

End your day by visiting orchards or produce stands. This is an especially enjoyable day for children—consider taking them to a county fair so they may see the animals, canned goods, and vegetables, all of which have special meaning to Diana.

November 29: St. Andrew's Eve

The night before St. Andrew's feast day was one of the most magical nights of the year in central and eastern Europe years ago. For centuries, all types of magic and divinations have been performed on this night. In many ways St. Andrew's Eve was similar to what Valentine's Day is in the West. Various forms of love magic were performed, including romantic spells, and many sought to induce prophetic dreams to reveal a future lover. And on this night, a knock at the door usually went unanswered because, according to legend, this was the only night of the year when vampires walked the countryside.

Magic and fortune-telling of all kinds were performed by candlelight on this magical eve. This would be the perfect night to scry using a black mirror, a dark water-filled bowl, or the surface of a lake or pond.

December/January

26 Monday
4th ♏
Color: Ivory

27 Tuesday
4th ♏
☽ v/c 2:26 am
Color: Scarlet

*Good stones for healing spells include
amethyst, malachite, peridot, ruby, and turquoise*

28 Wednesday
4th ♏
☽ enters ♐ 3:43 am
Color: Topaz

29 Thursday
4th ♐
☽ v/c 10:01 pm
Color: White

☽ Friday
4th ♐
☽ enters ♑ 6:35 am
New Moon 10:12 pm
Color: Purple

*To honor Venus and attract
love, wear rose, cedar, or cypress oil*

Set in Eastern Standard Time (EST)

31 Saturday

1st ♑

☽ v/c 4:09 am

Color: Black

1 Sunday

1st ♑

☽ enters ♒ 7:14 am

♀ enters ♑ 3:18 pm

Color: Yellow

Kwanzaa ends

New Year's Day

Birthday of Sir James Frazer,

author of *The Golden Bough*, 1854

January

2 Monday
1st ≈
Color: Gray

Hanukkah ends

3 Tuesday
1st ≈
☽ v/c 6:44 am
☽ enters ♓ 7:43 am
☿ enters ♑ 4:26 pm
Color: Red

Death of Edgar Cayce, psychic, 1945

4 Wednesday
1st ♓
Color: Brown

Aquarian Tabernacle Church
registered in Australia by
Lady Tamara Von Forslun, 1994

5 Thursday
1st ♓
☽ v/c 7:10 am
☽ enters ♈ 9:44 am
Color: Green

☽ Friday
1st ♈
2nd quarter 1:56 pm
Color: White

Twelfth Night/Epiphany
Patricia Crowther's witchcraft
radio show, *A Spell of Witchcraft*,
airs in Britain, 1971

Spokes and Spirals

Time spins slowly,
Holding us in its spiral,
Ever evolving.
We dance the seasons and the
Hours. We sing the Moon's changes.
Each day brings new lessons.
Each month means new magic.
Let them come, let them go.
Open yourself to the spin.
Free the mind, and
The heart must follow.
Hear the Moon's melody
Echoing, time turning toward the
Yoke of death and rebirth.
Embrace transformation.
All things, in the end,
Return to the Source.

—Elizabeth Barrette

---

7 Saturday
2nd ♈
☽ v/c 9:34 am
☽ enters ♉ 2:09 pm
Color: Blue

Increase your psychic power
with essential oils such as anise,
heliotrope, lilac, nutmeg, or sandalwood

---

8 Sunday
2nd ♉
Color: Orange

Birthday of MacGregor Mathers,
one of the three original founders
of the Golden Dawn, 1854
Death of Dion Fortune, 1946

January

9 Monday

2nd ♉
☽ v/c 1:56 pm
☽ enters ♊ 8:58 pm
Color: Lavender

Jamie Dodge wins lawsuit against
the Salvation Army, which fired her
based on her Wiccan religion, 1989

10 Tuesday

2nd ♊
Color: White

11 Wednesday

2nd ♊
☽ v/c 8:46 pm
Color: Yellow

*Tourmalinated quartz balances masculine and
feminine, subconscious and conscious aspects*

12 Thursday

2nd ♊
☽ enters ♋ 5:50 am
Color: Turquoise

Mary Smith hanged in England;
she had quarreled with neighbors,
who said that the Devil appeared
to her as a black man, 1616

13 Friday

2nd ♋
Color: Pink

Final witchcraft laws
repealed in Austria, 1787

Set in Eastern Standard Time (EST)

Cold Moon

The first lunar cycle after midwinter is known as the Cold Moon. This lunation corresponds to the Rowan Moon of Celtic traditions, and both echo the themes of introspection.

The winters past of not-so-long-ago meant long dark nights, scarcity of food, and a life lived indoors illuminated only by fire. We can easily imagine one of our ancestors wrapped in a thick fur hide, sitting near a hearth fire by night, staring mesmerized into the flames that meant the difference between survival and death. The full Cold Moon was a welcome light as it fell across the blue-white landscape.

While gazing into your own Cold Moon ritual fire, ask the Cailleach, the crone Goddess of the Celtic winter, to guide your introspections from daydreams to realized magic.

> *Cailleach, lady of icy blue,*
> *Bless the flames and show me true;*
> *Where am I going? What must I do?*
> *Cailleach, lady of icy blue.*

—Edain McCoy

☺ Saturday

2nd ♋
☽ v/c 4:48 am
3rd quarter 4:48 am
✳ D 5:51 am
☽ enters ♌ 4:31 pm
Color: Indigo

Cold Moon
Human Be-In, a Pagan-style festival,
takes place in San Francisco, attended by
Timothy Leary and Allen Ginsburg, 1967

---

15 Sunday

3rd ♌
Color: Gold

January

16 Monday
3rd ♌
☽ v/c 7:35 pm
Color: White

Birthday of Martin Luther King, Jr. (observed)
Birthday of Dr. Dennis Carpenter,
Circle Sanctuary

17 Tuesday
3rd ♌
☽ enters ♍ 4:49 am
Color: Black

18 Wednesday
3rd ♍
Color: Topaz

19 Thursday
3rd ♍
☽ v/c 5:12 pm
☽ enters ♎ 5:49 pm
Color: Purple

Birthday of Dorothy Clutterbuck,
who initiated Gerald Gardner, 1880

20 Friday
3rd ♎
☉ enters ♒ 12:15 am
Color: Rose

Sun enters Aquarius

Set in Eastern Standard Time (EST)

Darkling Mirror

Magic pools
In the witching hour,
Deeper than sleep.
Name it as you name yourself,
Instant of awareness
Glimpsed in dark glass.
How you choose to use
This knowledge is up to you.
                    —Elizabeth Barrette

---

21 Saturday
3rd ♎
Color: Brown

Celtic Tree Month of Rowan begins

◯ Sunday
3rd ♎
☽ v/c 3:53 am
☽ enters ♏ 5:28 am
4th quarter 10:14 am
☿ enters ♒ 3:41 pm
Color: Amber

Wear citrus scents like lemon on
Sunday to honor the Sun and lift your spirits

---

23 Monday
4th ♏
☽ v/c 4:53 pm
Color: Silver

Herbs for preventing theft
include caraway, garlic, and juniper

24 Tuesday
4th ♏
☽ enters ♐ 1:38 pm
Color: Gray

25 Wednesday
4th ♐
Color: White

Birthday of Robert Burns, Scottish poet, 1759

26 Thursday
4th ♐
☽ v/c 10:24 am
☽ enters ♑ 5:31 pm
Color: Crimson

27 Friday
4th ♑
Color: Purple

Brigid's Fresh Herbed Cheese

4 cloves garlic, minced
1 tsp. salt
¼ cup any fresh herbs, minced
    (blend any: rosemary, chives, dill,
    parsley, sage, thyme, chervil, basil)
8 oz. cream cheese
½ cup sour cream
¼ cup heavy cream
8 oz. small-curd cottage cheese

Make a paste with garlic, salt, and herbs. Beat the cream cheese until fluffy and, while beating, add first the creams and then the cottage cheese. Beat in the herbs until well blended.

    Line a colander with 2 layers of cheesecloth and spoon in cheese. Knot opposite corners and suspend over a bowl to drain for 24 hours (or hang over the faucet to drip in the sink). Retie as needed to compact the cheese. Remove to a plate, seam side down, and chill until serving. Can be rolled in fresh chopped parsley and served with water crackers.

—K. D. Spitzer

28 Saturday

4th ♑
☽ v/c 2:57 am
☽ enters ♒ 6:09 pm
Color: Black

If you break open an egg and it has two yolks,
someone you know will get married soon

☽ Sunday

4th ♒
New Moon 9:15 am
Color: Orange

Chinese New Year (dog)

January/February

30 Monday

1st ♒
☽ v/c 11:00 am
☽ enters ♓ 5:32 pm
Color: Ivory

Birthday of Zsusanna Budapest,
feminist Witch

31 Tuesday

1st ♓
Color: Maroon

Islamic New Year

Dr. Fian, believed to be the head
of the North Berwick Witches, found
guilty and executed for witchcraft in
Scotland by personal order of King
James VI (James I of England), 1591

1 Wednesday

1st ♓
☽ v/c 11:06 am
☽ enters ♈ 5:46 pm
Color: Yellow

2 Thursday

1st ♈
Color: Green

Imbolc
Groundhog Day
Leo Martello becomes a third-degree
Welsh traditionalist, 1973

3 Friday

1st ♈
♀ D 4:18 am
☽ v/c 1:33 pm
☽ enters ♉ 8:31 pm
Color: White

Imbolc crossquarter day
(Sun reaches 15° Aquarius)

Set in Eastern Standard Time (EST)

Imbolc

At Imbolc we mark the halfway point between winter and spring. Imbolc is a fire festival, and at this time of waxing light we call upon our own inner fire and work for inspiration, healing, and illumination. This Sabbat has several other popular names, including Candlemas and Brigid's Day.

Brigid is a Celtic goddess of the hearth and home and a favorite goddess of Witches, Pagans, and Druids. She is dearly loved as the patron of poetry, healing, and transformation. During this sabbat, why not work a little fire magic with Brigid and see what she may bring to your life?

Light a new white candle. Once the candle flame is burning bright and strong, repeat the charm three times.

> Brigid, goddess of poetry, health, and fire,
> On your special day, grant my inner desire.
> Your sacred flames bring light to me in so many ways,
> Please send inspiration and passion to me this day.

Watch over your spell candle until it goes out on its own.

—Ellen Dugan

---

4 Saturday

1st ♉
Color: Brown

Wear brown when you need security and stability; it makes you seem more reasonable to others, too

---

○ Sunday

1st ♉
2nd quarter 1:29 am
☽ v/c 4:00 pm
Color: Yellow

February

6 Monday
2nd ♉
☽ enters ♊ 2:32 am
Color: Lavender

7 Tuesday
2nd ♊
Color: Red

Death of Thomas Aquinas, scholar who
wrote that heresy was a product of
ignorance and therefore criminal, and
who refuted the *Canon Episcopi*, 1274

8 Wednesday
2nd ♊
♀ enters ♑ 7:00 am
☽ v/c 10:04 am
☽ enters ♋ 11:33 am
☿ enters ♓ 8:22 pm
Color: Brown

Birthday of Susun Weed, owner of
Wise Woman Publishing
Birthday of Evangeline Adams,
American astrologer, 1868

9 Thursday
2nd ♋
Color: White

10 Friday
2nd ♋
☽ v/c 3:53 pm
☽ enters ♌ 10:44 pm
Color: Pink

Zsusanna Budapest arrested and later
convicted for fortunetelling, 1975

Set in Eastern Standard Time (EST)

Quickening Moon

The Quickening Moon prods us to look inside ourselves for dormant possibilities. Our fellow creatures who sleep deep in the womb of Mother Earth are also feeling this pull as they are lulled into the hazy dreamland that prepares them for reawakening.

In western Europe this lunation heralded the cycle of birthing new lambs—the first tangible sign of the much-anticipated abundance of food in a world still ruled by cold and darkness.

To find our balance we must find the inner foundation on which we can build the lives we desire. Quickening Moon rituals can draw out the potential that now lies dormant in you. You may not know what marvels lie in wait, but they are there and are aching to awaken.

> *Stirring embers 'neath dark logs blaze,*
> *Sparks of life peek through smoke's haze;*
> *Likewise, in my soul, is potential untold,*
> *Break loose my soul to make potential unfold.*

—Edain McCoy

---

11 Saturday

2nd ♌
Color: Gray

☺ Sunday

2nd ♌
Full Moon 11:44 pm
Color: Gold

Quickening Moon

Gerald Gardner, founder of the Gardnerian tradition, dies of heart failure, 1964

February

13 Monday
3rd ♌
☽ v/c 6:48 am
☽ enters ♍ 11:13 am
Color: Gray

14 Tuesday
3rd ♍
Color: Black

Valentine's Day
Elsie Blum, a farmhand from
Oberstedten, Germany, sentenced
to death for witchcraft, 1652

15 Wednesday
3rd ♍
☽ v/c 10:21 pm
Color: White

Pope Leo X issues bull to ensure that the
secular courts carry out executions of
Witches convicted by the Inquisition,
1521; the bull was a response to the courts'
refusal to carry out the work of the Church

16 Thursday
3rd ♍
☽ enters ♎ 12:09 am
Color: Purple

17 Friday
3rd ♎
♂ enters ♊ 5:44 pm
Color: Rose

Three things which the careful person gains:
respect, plenty, and contentment

18 Saturday

3rd ♎
☽ v/c 11:59 am
☽ enters ♏ 12:11 pm
☉ enters ♓ 2:25 pm
Color: Blue

Sun enters Pisces
Celtic Tree Month of Ash begins

19 Sunday

3rd ♏
Color: Amber

February

20 Monday

3rd ♏
☽ v/c 5:02 am
☽ enters ♐ 9:38 pm
Color: Silver

Presidents' Day (observed)

Society for Psychical Research, devoted to paranormal research, founded in London, 1882

◑ Tuesday

3rd ♐
4th quarter 2:17 am
Color: White

Birthday of Patricia Telesco, Wiccan author

Stewart Farrar initiated into Alexandrian Wicca, 1970

Death of Theodore Parker Mills, 1996

22 Wednesday

4th ♐
☽ v/c 9:06 pm
Color: Topaz

Birthday of ShadowCat, Wiccan author

Birthday of Sybil Leek, Wiccan author, 1922

23 Thursday

4th ♐
☽ enters ♑ 3:16 am
⚳ D 8:04 am
Color: Turquoise

24 Friday

4th ♑
☽ v/c 7:58 pm
Color: Coral

Hidden by Light

Deep in the month,
A time of rest
Recharges before renewal.
Know this mystery, then:
Maiden, mother, crone
Only cover three quarters.
On the fourth is the unborn,
Not night but day veiling her face.
                    —Elizabeth Barrette

---

25 Saturday
4th ♑
☽ enters ♒ 5:14 am
♃ enters ♒ 5:49 am
Color: Indigo

---

26 Sunday
4th ♒
☽ v/c 11:25 pm
Color: Orange

Water rules many herbs, including
chamomile, licorice, rose, spearmint,
thyme, wintergreen, and yarrow

February/March

☽ Monday
4th ♒
☽ enters ♓ 4:56 am
New Moon 7:31 pm
Color: Ivory

Pope John XXII issues first bull to discuss
the practice of witchcraft, 1318

Birthday of Rudolph Steiner,
philosopher and father of the
biodynamic farming movement, 1861

28 Tuesday
1st ♓
☽ v/c 11:14 pm
Color: Scarlet

Mardi Gras

1 Wednesday
1st ♓
☽ enters ♈ 4:18 am
Color: Brown

Ash Wednesday
Preliminary hearings in the
Salem Witch trials held, 1692
Birthday of the Golden Dawn, 1888
Covenant of the Goddess (COG) formed, 1975

2 Thursday
1st ♈
☿ ℞ 3:29 pm
Color: White

3 Friday
1st ♈
☽ v/c 2:42 am
☽ enters ♉ 5:22 am
Color: Pink

Cranes are the messengers of the gods,
symbolizing immortality and happiness;
it's good luck if they nest near your house

Set in Eastern Standard Time (EST)

4 Saturday

1st ♉
♃ ℞ 1:02 pm
Color: Gray

Church of All Worlds incorporates in
Missouri, 1968, becoming the first Pagan
church to incorporate in the U.S.

5 Sunday

1st ♉
☽ v/c 3:14 am
♀ enters ♒ 3:39 am
☽ enters ♊ 9:37 am
Color: Gold

March

◐ Monday
1st ♊
2nd quarter 3:16 pm
Color: White

Birthday of Laurie Cabot, Wiccan author

7 Tuesday
2nd ♊
☽ v/c 11:09 am
☽ enters ♋ 5:38 pm
Color: Red

William Butler Yeats initiated
into the Isis-Urania Temple
of the Golden Dawn, 1890

8 Wednesday
2nd ♋
Color: Yellow

*Moldavite, a green meteorite,
channels healing energy and aids
communication with the higher self*

9 Thursday
2nd ♋
☽ v/c 3:41 pm
Color: Green

10 Friday
2nd ♋
☽ enters ♌ 4:42 am
Color: Purple

Date recorded for first meeting of
Dr. John Dee and Edward Kelly, 1582

Dutch clairvoyant and psychic
healer Gerard Croiser born, 1909

Set in Eastern Standard Time (EST)

Ostara Seed Bread

1 egg
1 cup buttermilk
⅓ cup vegetable oil
1 cup all-purpose flour
1 cup whole wheat flour
1 cup packed brown sugar
⅓ cup finely chopped walnuts
⅓ cup sliced almonds
2 tbs. each squash, flax, sesame,
  poppy, and celery seeds
1 tsp. baking powder
1 tsp. baking soda
½ tsp. salt

Combine egg, buttermilk, and oil; mix well. In a separate bowl, combine the dry ingredients; add to wet mixture, stirring well.

Spread in greased 9 x 5 inch loaf pan and bake in preheated 350°F oven for 50 to 60 minutes until tester comes out clean. Cool in pan for 10 minutes; turn out on a rack to cool.

Different seeds and nuts can be substituted; just be certain to use the same total amount given. Serve hot with honey butter or raspberry butter.

—K. D. Spitzer

11 Saturday
2nd ♌
Color: Brown

12 Sunday
2nd ♌
☽ v/c 10:38 am
☽ enters ♍ 5:23 pm
Color: Yellow

Stewart Edward White, psychic researcher, born, 1873; he later became president of the American Society for Psychical Research in San Francisco

March

13 Monday

2nd ♍
Color: Silver

Three things hard to do:
cool the fire, dry the water, and please the world

☺ Tuesday

2nd ♍
Full Moon 6:35 pm
☽ v/c 11:33 pm
Color: Black

Purim
Storm Moon
Lunar eclipse 6:49 pm, 24° ♍ 15'

15 Wednesday

3rd ♍
☽ enters ♎ 6:12 am
Color: White

Pete Pathfinder Davis becomes the first
Wiccan priest elected as president of the
Interfaith Council of Washington State, 1995

16 Thursday

3rd ♎
Color: Purple

17 Friday

3rd ♎
☽ v/c 11:31 am
☽ enters ♏ 5:59 pm
Color: Coral

St. Patrick's Day
Eleanor Shaw and Mary Phillips executed
in England for bewitching a woman
and her two children, 1705

Set in Eastern Standard Time (EST)

Storm Moon

The old adage tells us, "March comes in like a lion and goes out like a lamb." In North America, where the world's largest concentration of electrical storms occur, we might not see that lamb until June. During this cycle we are more likely to focus on personal safety rather than the magical potential of cyclones. But the two need not be mutually exclusive.

Include a few magical tools in your storm kit. After securing property, pets, and loved ones, you can be together as a family, warding your home and one another from danger. While in the safety of your storm shelter, you can use the counterclockwise energy of the cyclone to help you connect to the attributes of erasing negatives from your lives, thus eliminating your inner—as well as your outer—storms.

Get a jump on the dangers of a North American spring by gathering everyone in your household to the family altar on the Storm Moon to weave a spell of protection around your home and all who dwell within.

—Edain McCoy

---

18 Saturday
3rd ♏
Color: Blue

Celtic Tree Month of Alder begins
Birthday of Edgar Cayce, psychic researcher, 1877

19 Sunday
3rd ♏
Color: Orange

Elizabethan statute against witchcraft enacted, 1563; this statute was replaced in 1604 by a stricter one from King James I

March

20 Monday
3rd ♏

☽ v/c 2:54 am
☽ enters ♐ 3:43 am
☉ enters ♈ 1:25 pm
Color: Lavender

Ostara/Spring Equinox
Sun enters Aries
International Astrology Day
Death of Lady Sheba, author
of *The Book of Shadows*, 2002

21 Tuesday
3rd ♐
Color: Gray

Mandate of Henry VIII against witchcraft enacted, 1542; repealed in 1547
Green Egg magazine founded, 1968

○ Wednesday
3rd ♐

☽ v/c 4:47 am
☽ enters ♑ 10:36 am
4th quarter 2:10 pm
Color: Topaz

Pope Clement urged by Phillip IV
to suppress Templar order, 1311

23 Thursday
4th ♑

☽ v/c 6:30 pm
Color: Crimson

24 Friday
4th ♑

☽ enters ♒ 2:21 pm
Color: White

Birthday of Alyson Hannigan, who played
Willow on *Buffy the Vampire Slayer*
Arrest of Florence Newton, one of the
few Witches burned in Ireland, 1661

Ostara

The Vernal Equinox is the beginning of the spring season. This festival's familiar symbols of rabbits, pastel-colored eggs, and bright spring flowers are sweet and romantic. Look around you: everywhere in nature there are signs of life returning to the land. To bring a bit of this natural magic indoors, pick up a pretty pot of blooming bulbs. Try tulips for love, or daffodils for chivalry and honor, and take them home to brighten things up. Perhaps you can jazz them up a little by tucking some moss over the soil or adding a festive bow or tiny colored eggs to the container. Enchant these spring flowers for fresh starts and good luck. Light a soft green candle and call on the goddess of spring, Eostre, to work this sabbat spell for new beginnings and to increase the positive things in your life.

> *Ostara begins our season of spring,*
> *Good luck, joy, and cheer these flowers do bring.*
> *Eostre, bless my home, family, and friends,*
> *May your love and blessings never end.*

—Ellen Dugan

---

25 Saturday

4th ≈
☿ D 8:42 am
Color: Indigo

Innocent III issues bull to
establish the Inquisition, 1199

---

26 Sunday

4th ≈
☽ v/c 10:18 am
☽ enters ♓ 3:33 pm
Color: Amber

Birthday of Joseph Campbell, author
and professor of mythology, 1910

March/April

27 Monday
4th ♓
Color: Ivory

When giving someone a purse or wallet, put a
coin inside; the recipient will grow in prosperity

28 Tuesday
4th ♓
✳ enters ♋ 6:59 am
☽ v/c 10:20 am
☽ enters ♈ 3:31 pm
Color: White

Scott Cunningham dies of
complications caused by AIDS, 1993

☿ Wednesday
4th ♈
New Moon 5:15 am
♇ ℞ 7:40 am
Color: Yellow

Solar eclipse 5:33 am, 08° ♈ 35'

30 Thursday
1st ♈
☽ v/c 10:41 am
☽ enters ♉ 4:00 pm
Color: Turquoise

31 Friday
1st ♉
Color: Rose

Last Witch trial in Ireland,
held at Magee Island, 1711

Set in Eastern Standard Time (EST)

Signs of Life

Season of renewal,
Persephone returning like
Rising sap to burst buds
Into blossoms—everywhere we
Notice the signs of life
Getting on with itself.
　　　　　　—Elizabeth Barrette

---

1 Saturday

1st ♉
☽ v/c 10:52 am
☽ enters ♊ 6:49 pm
Color: Black

April Fools' Day

---

2 Sunday

1st ♊
Color: Yellow

Daylight Saving Time begins at 2 am

April

3 Monday

1st ♊
☽ v/c 10:24 pm
Color: Gray

4 Tuesday

1st ♊
☽ enters ♋ 2:15 am
Color: White

*Iron protects against malicious
entities, and a nail found by
chance serves better than one bought*

◐ Wednesday

1st ♋
2nd quarter 8:01 am
♄ D 8:54 am
☽ v/c 1:19 pm
♀ enters ♓ 9:21 pm
Color: Topaz

Trial of Alice Samuel, her
husband, and daughter, who
were accused of bewitching the
wife of Sir Henry Cromwell and
several village children, 1593

6 Thursday

2nd ♋
☽ enters ♌ 12:25 pm
Color: Green

7 Friday

2nd ♌
Color: Pink

Church of All Worlds founded, 1962
First Wiccan "tract" published
by Pete Pathfinder Davis, 1996

8 Saturday

2nd ♌
☽ v/c 7:02 pm
Color: Brown

William Alexander Aynton initiated into
the Isis-Urania temple of the Golden
Dawn, 1896; he would later be called the
"Grand Old Man" of the Golden Dawn

9 Sunday

2nd ♌
☽ enters ♍ 12:58 am
Color: Amber

Palm Sunday

April

10 Monday
2nd ♍
Color: Silver

Birthday of Rev. Montague Summers,
orthodox scholar and author of *A
History of Witchcraft and Demonology*, 1880

11 Tuesday
2nd ♍
☽ v/c 10:59 am
☽ enters ♎ 1:46 pm
Color: Red

Burning of Major Weir, Scottish "sorcerer"
who confessed of his own accord, 1670;
some historians believe that the major
became delusional or senile because up
until his confession he had an excellent
reputation and was a pillar of society

12 Wednesday
2nd ♎
Color: Yellow

☺ Thursday
2nd ♎
Full Moon 12:40 pm
☽ v/c 6:42 pm
♂ enters ♋ 8:59 pm
Color: Purple

Passover begins
Wind Moon

14 Friday
3rd ♎
☽ enters ♏ 1:08 am
Color: Coral

Good Friday
Adoption of the Principles of
Wiccan Belief at "Witch Meet"
in St. Paul, Minnesota, 1974

Set in Eastern Daylight Time (EDT)

Wind Moon

The Wind or Seed Moon of April is Moon-drenched ritual foreplay. Capricious spring winds dance their fertility rite, scattering seeds that root miles from their birthplaces. With the randy sabbat of Beltane close on our heels, we easily imagine the young God and Goddess awakening to the power and excitement of their impending divine marriage—a sexual union allowing life to flourish for another year. Picture these two bewitching bare-bodied beings lying together in a woodland grotto, hands and lips exploring new possibilities of pleasure and creation—both gifts they have given to us. Sadly, many of our fellow human beings have deemed this gift perverse, shunned except for the necessity of procreation. Or is that pro-creation?

We cannot deny the innate attraction of two halves of a whole finding and uniting with one another. We are cast in the image of our deities, and under the Wind Moon we find ourselves in tune with the newborn Earth and awaken with her to the many things we can create when we meet our other half.

—Edain McCoy

---

15 Saturday

3rd ♏
☽ v/c 2:29 pm
Color: Blue

Celtic Tree Month of Willow begins
Birthday of Elizabeth Montgomery,
who played Samantha on *Bewitched*, 1933

---

16 Sunday

3rd ♏
☿ enters ♈ 8:20 am
☽ enters ♐ 10:19 am
Color: Gold

Easter
Birthday of Margot Adler, author
of *Drawing Down the Moon*

April

17 Monday
3rd ♐
Color: Ivory

Aleister Crowley breaks into and takes over the
Golden Dawn temple, providing the catalyst for
the demise of the original Golden Dawn, 1900

18 Tuesday
3rd ♐
☽ v/c 2:41 pm
☽ enters ♑ 5:13 pm
Color: Black

19 Wednesday
3rd ♑
☽ v/c 9:15 pm
Color: Brown

Passover ends

Conviction of Witches at
second of four famous trials at
Chelmsford, England, 1579

☽ Thursday
3rd ♑
☉ enters ♉ 1:26 am
☽ enters ♒ 9:56 pm
4th quarter 11:28 pm
Color: Crimson

Sun enters Taurus

21 Friday
4th ♒
Color: Purple

Orthodox Good Friday

Set in Eastern Daylight Time (EDT)

Breakthrough

Day breaks like an egg,
A golden yolk of Sun shining through
White cloud, reminding us of this magic:
No darkness lasts forever.

     —Elizabeth Barrette

---

22 Saturday

4th ≈

☽ v/c 7:03 pm

Color: Gray

Earth Day; the first Earth Day was in 1970

---

23 Sunday

4th ≈

☽ enters ♓ 12:43 am

Color: Orange

Orthodox Easter

Edward III of England begins the
Order of the Garter, 1350

First National All-Woman Conference on
Women's Spirituality held, Boston, 1976

April

24 Monday
4th ♓
☽ v/c 8:35 pm
Color: Lavender

25 Tuesday
4th ♓
☽ enters ♈ 2:12 am
Color: Scarlet

*USA Today reports that Patricia Hutchins is
the first military Wiccan granted religious
leave for the sabbats, 1989*

26 Wednesday
4th ♈
☽ v/c 9:44 pm
Color: White

*Wear white when you need to
meditate, teach, or resolve a dispute*

☽ Thursday
4th ♈
☽ enters ♉ 3:27 am
New Moon 3:44 pm
Color: Turquoise

28 Friday
1st ♉
☽ v/c 9:31 pm
Color: Rose

*Three reasons for speaking, come what may:
instruction against ignorance, counsel
against strife, truth against harmful lies*

Bel's Asparagus Avec Amour

16 thin asparagus spears
1 tbs. butter
3 eggs
3 tbs. heavy cream
1 tbs. freshly chopped chives
1 tbs. slivers of smoked salmon
1 tbs. ground walnuts

Prepare asparagus by snapping each spear and discarding the lower end.
Pare if necessary. Blanch in salted water for 2 to 3 minutes. Keep warm and
dress with a dab of butter. Divide into two portions.

    Melt tablespoon of butter and beat eggs, cream, chives, and half the
salmon together. Cook mixture in butter until softly scrambled. Spoon
over asparagus and garnish with salt and pepper and remaining salmon.
Dust with ground walnuts. Asparagus spears can be arranged on thin slices
of a good, toasted artisan bread. Serves you and your beloved a light
Beltane midnight meal of aphrodisiacs.

—K .D. Spitzer

---

29 Saturday
1st ♉
☽ enters ♊ 5:58 am
Color: Indigo

Birthday of Ed Fitch, Wiccan author

---

30 Sunday
1st ♊
Color: Yellow

Walpurgis Night; traditionally the
German Witches gather on the Blocksberg,
a mountain in northeastern Germany

May

1 Monday

1st ♊
☽ v/c 7:13 am
☽ enters ♋ 11:17 am
Color: White

Beltane/May Day
Order of the Illuminati formed in
Bavaria by Adam Weishaupt, 1776

2 Tuesday

1st ♋
Color: Black

Birthday of D. J. Conway, Wiccan author

3 Wednesday

1st ♋
♀ enters ♈ 6:24 am
☽ v/c 2:35 pm
☽ enters ♌ 8:18 pm
Color: Yellow

4 Thursday

1st ♌
Color: Purple

The *New York Herald Tribune*
carries the story of a woman who
brought her neighbor to court on
a charge of bewitchment, 1895

◐ Friday

1st ♌
2nd quarter 1:13 am
☿ enters ♉ 4:28 am
Color: Coral

Cinco de Mayo
Beltane crossquarter day
(Sun reaches 15° Taurus)

Set in Eastern Daylight Time (EDT)

Beltane

Got the urge to grow your very own Witch's garden? Beltane is a great time of the year to start your herbal magic off with a real kick. Gather your plants, seeds, and gardening supplies, and bless the plants for luxuriant growth, gorgeous blooms, and healthy foliage.

This charm will work for any size or style of garden. Sit or stand within the garden, or next to the new flowers and plants. Then hold your hands out, palms turned up, and repeat the charm. Call on the Lord and the Lady to assist you. At this time of the year their passionate energy will flow into all living things.

> *If you plant your herbs and flowers at the start of May.*
> *Then whisper this Garden Witch's charm on Beltane day,*
> *"I enchant these green plants for power, and magic true,*
> *Lord and Lady bless my herb-craft, and all that I do."*

After the charm is complete, turn your hands over and visualize all that magic flowing from your hands and into the garden plants. Happy magical gardening!

—Ellen Dugan

---

6 Saturday

2nd ♌
☽ v/c 1:01 am
☽ enters ♍ 8:20 am
Color: Brown

Long Island Church of Aphrodite
formed by Reverend Gleb Botkin, 1938

---

7 Sunday

2nd ♍
☿ ℞ 9:28 am
Color: Orange

Pyrite, a golden metallic ore,
represents the power of the Sun

May

8 Monday
2nd ♍
☽ v/c 1:49 pm
☽ enters ♎ 9:10 pm
Color: Lavender

Wear the color lavender to relax;
it brings awareness of inner beauty

9 Tuesday
2nd ♎
Color: Scarlet

Joan of Arc canonized, 1920
First day of the Lemuria, a Roman
festival of the dead; this festival
was probably borrowed from the
Etruscans and is one possible
ancestor of our modern Halloween

10 Wednesday
2nd ♎
Color: Brown

11 Thursday
2nd ♎
☽ v/c 1:15 am
☽ enters ♏ 8:24 am
Color: White

Massachusetts Bay Colony Puritans
ban Christmas celebrations
because they are too pagan, 1659

12 Friday
2nd ♏
Color: Pink

Flower Moon

April showers bring May flowers. In Europe and North America, Pagans dance beneath the Moon and celebrate the marriage of our God and Goddess. The Earth has reawakened in her full beauty with flowers bursting up from beneath our feet, tempting us to find our mates with their gentle blend of exotic scents.

Freed from the confinements of winter, the erotic allure of the smell of rich earth and new growth has always tempted lovers to mate near soft spring grasses and rows of floral beauty.

> April showers bring May flowers,
> At least that's what they say;
> May flowers, a bed of softest bowers,
> Where my love and I can play.
> God of the Moon and of the May,
> Tempt my love to me this way,
> With the Goddess of Flowers scented to swoon,
> Find me with my love under the Flower Moon.

—Edain McCoy

☺ Saturday

2nd ♏
☽ v/c 2:51 am
Full Moon 2:51 am
☽ enters ♐ 4:56 pm
Color: Blue

Flower Moon
Celtic Tree Month of Hawthorn begins

---

14 Sunday

3rd ♐
Color: Amber

Mother's Day
Widow Robinson of Kidderminster
and her two daughters are arrested for
trying to prevent the return of Charles II
from exile by use of magic, 1660

May

15 Monday

3rd ♐
♀ ℞ 4:37 am
☽ v/c 4:15 pm
☽ enters ♑ 10:59 pm
Color: Gray

Three things which we cannot control:
time, space, and truth

16 Tuesday

3rd ♑
Color: Red

Census Day (Canada)

17 Wednesday

3rd ♑
☽ v/c 10:10 pm
Color: White

18 Thursday

3rd ♑
☽ enters ♒ 3:19 am
Color: Turquoise

Thursday's gem is rose quartz;
use it to mend hurt feelings

19 Friday

3rd ♒
☿ enters ♊ 4:52 pm
Color: Purple

Set in Eastern Daylight Time (EDT)

◖ **Saturday**

3rd ♒
☽ v/c 5:20 am
4th quarter 5:20 am
☽ enters ♓ 6:39 am
Color: Indigo

21 Sunday

4th ♓
☉ enters ♊ 12:31 am
Color: Yellow

Sun enters Gemini
Birthday of Gwyddion Pendderwen,
Pagan bard, 1946

May

22 Monday
4th ♓
☽ v/c 2:45 am
♆ ℞ 9:05 am
☽ enters ♈ 9:24 am
Color: Silver

Adoption of the Earth Religion
Anti-Abuse Act, 1988

23 Tuesday
4th ♈
Color: Gray

Three things are excellent for a person:
valor, learning, and discretion

24 Wednesday
4th ♈
☽ v/c 5:16 am
☽ enters ♉ 12:00 pm
Color: Topaz

25 Thursday
4th ♉
Color: Crimson

Scott Cunningham initiated into
the Traditional Gwyddonic
Order of the Wicca, 1981

26 Friday
4th ♉
☽ v/c 6:39 am
☽ enters ♊ 3:19 pm
Color: White

Blackbirds perched in high places (such as
rooftops) foretell good weather; in low places
(like fenceposts) they foretell bad weather

Set in Eastern Daylight Time (EDT)

Wearing Her Cloak

Walk through fresh-tilled fields
And imagine you hear the
Xylophone chime of moonlight
In the mothering dark. This
Night makes magic, slow
Growing but strong, spells that
Mature as crescent becomes circle.
Over the open land like a cloak
Of opal silk she throws her power:
Naked, you may borrow it to wear.
                            —Elizabeth Barrette

☽ Saturday
4th ♊
New Moon 1:25 am
⚶ enters ♌ 6:31 am
Color: Black

Birthday of Morning Glory
Zell, Church of All Worlds

Final confession of witchcraft by
Isobel Gowdie, Scotland, 1662

---

28 Sunday
1st ♊
☽ v/c 7:23 pm
☽ enters ♋ 8:33 pm
Color: Gold

---

29 Monday

1st ♋
♀ enters ♉ 8:41 am
Color: Ivory

Memorial Day (observed)

30 Tuesday

1st ♋
Color: White

Death of Joan of Arc, 1431

31 Wednesday

1st ♋
☽ v/c 12:42 am
☽ enters ♌ 4:51 am
Color: Yellow

1 Thursday

1st ♌
Color: Green

Witchcraft Act of 1563
takes effect in England

2 Friday

1st ♌
☽ v/c 1:34 pm
☽ enters ♍ 4:17 pm
Color: Pink

Shavuot
Birthday of Alessandro
di Cagliostro, magician, 1743

☽ **Saturday**

1st ♍

☿ enters ♋ 7:21 am
♂ enters ♌ 2:43 pm
2nd quarter 7:06 pm
Color: Brown

*Herbs for air include anise, bergamot,
lavender, meadowsweet, and parsley*

4 **Sunday**

2nd ♍

☽ v/c 8:30 pm
Color: Orange

June

5 Monday

2nd ♍
☽ enters ♎ 5:08 am
☿ enters ♌ 5:33 am
Color: Lavender

6 Tuesday

2nd ♎
Color: Red

*Wear cardinal red to make yourself
feel and appear more desirable*

7 Wednesday

2nd ♎
☽ v/c 8:15 am
☽ enters ♏ 4:41 pm
Color: Topaz

8 Thursday

2nd ♏
Color: Purple

*Thursday's scent is patchouli;
wear it to remind yourself of wild places*

9 Friday

2nd ♏
☽ v/c 6:10 am
Color: White

Birthday of Grace Cook, medium and
founder of the White Eagle Lodge, 1892

Strong Sun Moon

The Full Moon of June rises in an eastern sky still bright with a strong western Sun. Under this Moon we celebrate the God's apex of strength with dance and song, aware that after the solstice, his power will begin to wane, and it is the Goddess—metaphorically pregnant with the fall harvest—who will dominate our lunar rites for the remainder of the year.

Acknowledge this time of lunar-solar balance by gathering an object sacred to each. Take the solar object and place it inside the ground as the Sun sets in the west. Facing east, give an offering of an object sacred to the Moon as she rises to rule the night sky once more.

Sinking Sun to your western domain,
To land of the dead from whence you came,
Make way now for our Moon, our queen,
Silver light of potential yet unseen.

—Edain McCoy

10 Saturday
2nd ♏
☽ enters ♐ 1:05 am
Color: Gray

Celtic Tree Month of Oak begins
Hanging of Bridget Bishop, first to
die in the Salem Witch trials, 1692

☺ Sunday
2nd ♐
Full Moon 2:03 pm
☽ v/c 10:34 pm
Color: Gold

Strong Sun Moon
James I Witchcraft Statute replaces the
1563 mandate with stricter penalties, 1604

June

12 Monday
3rd ♐
☽ enters ♑ 6:19 am
Color: Silver

13 Tuesday
3rd ♑
☽ v/c 12:50 pm
Color: Black

Birthday of William Butler Yeats, poet
and member of the Golden Dawn, 1865
Birthday of Gerald Gardner, founder
of the Gardnerian Tradition, 1884

14 Wednesday
3rd ♑
☽ enters ♒ 9:32 am
Color: Brown

Flag Day

15 Thursday
3rd ♒
Color: White

Margaret Jones becomes the first person executed
as a Witch in the Massachusetts Bay Colony,
1648; she was a Boston doctor who was accused of
witchcraft after several of her patients died

16 Friday
3rd ♒
☽ v/c 4:24 am
☽ enters ♓ 12:05 pm
Color: Rose

Set in Eastern Daylight Time (EDT)

Solstice Cookies

½ cup butter
¾ cup brown sugar
1 egg, slightly beaten
1½ tsp. vanilla
½ tsp. salt
½ cup flour
1 cup whole wheat flour
¾ tsp. baking powder
1½ cups rolled oats
¾ cup chopped apricots, dates, or raisins
½ cup toasted sunflower seeds
1 to 4 tbs. water (as needed)

Preheat oven to 375°F. Cream butter and sugar; add egg, vanilla, and salt, mixing well. Stir dry ingredients; mix everything together. Add water a tablespoon at a time until dough holds together. Drop on greased cookie sheet, flatten slightly, and bake 10 to 12 minutes. Makes about 3 dozen. Serve with Strawberry Rhubarb Punch. Simmer until tender: 3 cups chopped rhubarb in 3 cups water. Add a 6 oz. can frozen lemonade, 2 cans water and ¾ cup sugar. Strain and chill. Just before serving, add a quart of lemon/lime soda. Garnish with strawberries and lemon verbena.

—K. D. Spitzer

---

17 Saturday

3rd ♓
Color: Blue

Birthday of Starhawk, Wiccan author

◯ Sunday

3rd ♓
☽ v/c 10:08 am
4th quarter 10:08 am
☽ enters ♈ 2:54 pm
Color: Amber

Father's Day
Church of All Worlds
chartered with the IRS, 1970

19 Monday
4th ♈
♅ ℞ 3:40 am
Color: Gray

20 Tuesday
4th ♈
☽ v/c 5:20 pm
☽ enters ♉ 6:23 pm
Color: White

Three things necessary for each act:
desire, knowledge, and ability

21 Wednesday
4th ♉
☉ enters ♋ 8:26 am
Color: Yellow

Midsummer/Litha/Summer Solstice
Sun enters Cancer

22 Thursday
4th ♉
☽ v/c 8:44 pm
☽ enters ♊ 10:49 pm
Color: Crimson

Final witchcraft law in
England repealed, 1951

23 Friday
4th ♊
♀ enters ♊ 8:31 pm
Color: Purple

Litha

On the day of the Summer Solstice, slip outside for a few moments and quietly watch the Sun rise. Tip your face up to the light of the Sun on its mightiest day and soak up a little Sun magic. Tie a small piece of ribbon loosely onto the branch of an oak tree and make an unselfish wish for prosperity and health. Choose your ribbon's color with care, and keep it in the theme of the Summer Solstice. For example, you could use a gold ribbon for wealth and success, an orange ribbon for energy, a green ribbon for healing, or a yellow ribbon for cheer. Use this charm as you tie the ribbon on.

Tip your face up to the Sun's light today,
Remember the Old Gods in simple ways.
Tie a ribbon in the branches of the oak, so green,
And tonight, the faeries will show you things unseen.

Tonight take a walk in the garden and look for the faeries. Remember, by acknowledging the spirits of the land and keeping yourself tuned to its tides and seasons, you stand a much better chance of encountering the Fey.

—Ellen Dugan

---

24 Saturday

4th ♊
☽ v/c 8:02 pm
Color: Black

Birthday of Janet Farrar, Wiccan author
James I Witchcraft Statute of 1604 is replaced in 1763 with a law against pretending to practice divination and witchcraft; law stands until 1951

☽ Sunday

4th ♊
☽ enters ♋ 4:48 am
New Moon 12:05 pm
Color: Yellow

A law is introduced in Germany by Archbishop Siegfried III to encourage conversion rather than burning of heretics, 1233

June/July

26 Monday
1st ♋
Color: Ivory

Birthday of Stewart Farrar, Wiccan author

Richard of Gloucester assumes the English
throne after accusing the widowed
queen of Edward IV of witchcraft, 1483

27 Tuesday
1st ♋
☽ v/c 12:02 pm
☽ enters ♌ 1:09 pm
Color: Scarlet

Birthday of Scott Cunningham,
Wiccan author, 1956

28 Wednesday
1st ♌
☿ enters ♌ 3:57 pm
Color: White

29 Thursday
1st ♌
☽ v/c 2:24 pm
Color: Turquoise

*Moss agate helps you connect
with the forest and spirits of wilderness*

30 Friday
1st ♌
☽ enters ♍ 12:15 am
Color: Coral

Set in Eastern Daylight Time (EDT)

Ripe for the Picking

Soft breezes stir a thousand flowers
Under a turquoise sky. Birds sing.
Mothers show butterflies to their children.
Magic folds itself in dreamy layers,
Easy as heat waves on the horizon,
Ripe as corn for the picking.
                        —Elizabeth Barrette

---

1 Saturday
1st ♍
Color: Brown

---

2 Sunday
1st ♍
☽ v/c 2:58 am
☽ enters ♎ 1:06 pm
Color: Orange

*Yellow jasper represents the Sun at its
setting, and is a stone of contemplation
and gentle endings in their proper time*

July

◯ Monday

1st ♎
2nd quarter 12:37 pm
Color: Lavender

Trial of Joan Prentice, who was accused
of sending an imp in the form of a
ferret to bite children; she allegedly had
two imps named Jack and Jill, 1549

4 Tuesday

2nd ♎
☽ v/c 3:17 pm
☿ ℞ 3:33 pm
Color: Red

Independence Day

5 Wednesday

2nd ♎
☽ enters ♏ 1:13 am
Color: Yellow

Conviction of Witches at third of four
famous trials at Chelmsford, England, 1589

6 Thursday

2nd ♏
♃ D 3:19 am
☽ v/c 3:54 pm
Color: Green

Scott Cunningham is initiated into
the Ancient Pictish Gaelic Way, 1981

7 Friday

2nd ♏
☽ enters ♐ 10:13 am
Color: White

Set in Eastern Daylight Time (EDT)

8 Saturday
2nd ♐
Color: Gray

Celtic Tree Month of Holly

9 Sunday
2nd ♐
☽ v/c 6:31 am
☽ enters ♑ 3:25 pm
Color: Amber

Death of Herman Slater,
proprietor of Magickal Childe
bookstore in New York, 1992
Birthday of Amber K, Wiccan author

July

☺ Monday

2nd ♑

☿ enters ♋ 4:18 pm
Full Moon 11:02 pm
Color: White

Blessing Moon

11 Tuesday

3rd ♑

☽ v/c 4:58 pm
☽ enters ♒ 5:46 pm
Color: Black

A twig of thorns will protect a
house from danger, but must be
found loose, not cut from the tree

12 Wednesday

3rd ♒
Color: Brown

13 Thursday

3rd ♒

☽ v/c 10:23 am
☽ enters ♓ 6:59 pm
Color: Turquoise

Birthday of Dr. John Dee, magician, 1527

14 Friday

3rd ♓
Color: Pink

First crop circles recorded
on Silbury Hill, 1988

Set in Eastern Daylight Time (EDT)

Blessing Moon

The Moon illuminating the July night reassures us that the cycle of life is proceeding as it should. No matter how dark or uncertain the night, we can go to a window and see a pale yellow light falling across lush woodlands and growing fields. Mother Earth is still gestating the coming harvest, and as with any mother-to-be, we can't count on a successful birth until it has been gathered in and we can hold it in our hands and hearts.

Under the Blessing Moon, pause to tally up your own blessings—the ones you currently have, and those you hope to have in the near future. Write them down and allow the paper to remain out all night under the Full Moon. Be careful that not one ray of sunlight spills across your list. The Sun represents the self you show to the world, but the Moon represents your inner self. These are your private yearnings, and all good weavers of wishes know that keeping silent about your heart's desire is the quickest way to bring it to manifestation.

—Edain McCoy

---

15 Saturday

3rd ♓
☽ v/c 3:56 pm
☽ enters ♈ 8:39 pm
Color: Blue

*Lapis is the stone of truth; work
with it to enhance your ability
to detect lies and evasions*

---

16 Sunday

3rd ♈
Color: Gold

July

☽ Monday
3rd ♈
4th quarter 3:12 pm
☽ v/c 9:33 pm
☽ enters ♉ 11:44 pm
Color: Ivory

First airing of *The Witching Hour*, a
Pagan radio show hosted by Winter
Wren and Don Lewis, on station
WONX in Evanston, Illinois, 1992

18 Tuesday
4th ♉
♀ enters ♋ 10:41 pm
Color: Gray

19 Wednesday
4th ♉
Color: White

Rebecca Nurse hanged in
Salem, Massachusetts, 1692

20 Thursday
4th ♉
☽ v/c 1:48 am
☽ enters ♊ 4:38 am
Color: Crimson

Pope Adrian VI issues a bull to the
Inquisition to re-emphasize the 1503
bull of Julius II calling for the purging
of "sorcerers by fire and sword," 1523

21 Friday
4th ♊
Color: Rose

Three things hard to check:
the stream of a cataract, the arrow
from a bow, and the rash tongue

Set in Eastern Daylight Time (EDT)

Anvil of Hours

Now the Sun strikes
On its anvil of hours, forging power.
Open the oven's door if you dare, and
Name its fire your own.

                    —Elizabeth Barrette

---

22 Saturday

4th ♊
☽ v/c 11:17 am
☽ enters ♋ 11:28 am
♂ enters ♍ 2:53 pm
☉ enters ♌ 7:18 pm
Color: Indigo

Sun enters Leo
Northamptonshire Witches
condemned, 1612
First modern recorded sighting
of the Loch Ness Monster, 1930

---

23 Sunday

4th ♋
Color: Yellow

July

24 Monday
4th ♋
☽ v/c 5:07 am
☽ enters ♌ 8:24 pm
Color: Silver

The pink stone kunzite promotes
inner love and aids in self-discipline

Tuesday
4th ♌
New Moon 12:31 am
Color: Maroon

Death of Pope Innocent VIII, who issued
bull *Summis Desiderantes Affectibus*, 1492

---

26 Wednesday
1st ♌
☽ v/c 8:32 pm
Color: Topaz

Confession of Chelmsford Witches at first
of four famous trials at Chelmsford, 1566;
the others were held in 1579, 1589, and
1645; "Witch Finder General" Matthew
Hopkins presided at the 1645 trials

---

27 Thursday
1st ♌
☽ enters ♍ 7:36 am
Color: Purple

Jennet Preston becomes the first of the
"Malkin Tower" Witches to be hung; she
was convicted of hiring Witches to help
her murder Thomas Lister, 1612

---

28 Friday
1st ♍
☿ D 8:39 pm
Color: Coral

Lugh's Summer Corn Bisque

5 ears of corn (4 cups kernels)
½ onion, chopped
1 celery rib, chopped
1 bay leaf
½ cup heavy cream

Garnish:
12 scallops
1 tsp. each dried chives and dill

Cut kernels from ears; using dull side of knife, also scrape milk and meat from cob into bowl of corn. Break cobs in half and simmer in 6 cups water with vegetables and bay leaf for 15 minutes. Remove cobs. Reserve 1 cup of kernels; add rest to pot with cream and salt to taste. Simmer for 5 minutes; remove bay leaf and puree. Return to pot; add remaining corn and gently reheat. Do not boil. For the garnish, rub scallops with herbs and sauté in hot butter until cooked (1 to 2 minutes). Ladle soup in warmed bowls and garnish each with 3 scallops. Makes 4 servings.

—K. D. Spitzer

29 Saturday
1st ♍
☽ v/c 9:05 am
☽ enters ♎ 8:27 pm
Color: Black

Agnes Waterhouse, one of the Chelmsford Witches, is hanged under the new witchcraft statute of Elizabeth I, 1566; she was accused of having a spotted cat familiar named Sathan

30 Sunday
1st ♎
Color: Amber

Conrad of Marburg is murdered on the open road, presumably because he had shifted from persecuting poor heretics to nobles, 1233

July/August

31 Monday

1st ♎
☽ v/c 9:54 pm
Color: Gray

Birthday of H. P. Blavatsky, founder
of the Theosophical Society, 1831

Date of fabled meeting of British
Witches to raise cone of power to stop
Hitler's invasion of England, 1940

1 Tuesday

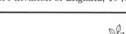

1st ♎
☽ enters ♏ 9:08 am
Color: White

Lammas/Lughnasadh
Birthday of Edward Kelly,
medium of Dr. John Dee, 1555
AURORA Network UK founded, 2000

◑ Wednesday

1st ♏
2nd quarter 4:46 am
Color: Yellow

Birthday of Henry Steele Olcott,
who cofounded the Theosophical
Society with H. P. Blavatsky, 1832

3 Thursday

2nd ♏
☽ v/c 5:08 am
☽ enters ♐ 7:13 pm
Color: Crimson

4 Friday

2nd ♐
☿ enters ♍ 1:08 am
Color: Pink

*Peppermint has powers of healing and
purification; it raises the energy of an area*

Set in Eastern Daylight Time (EDT)

Lughnasadh

Lughnasadh or Lammas is the first of three harvest festivals. Today we celebrate the beginning of the harvest season. As the earliest grains, fruits, and vegetables from the garden and summer berries are ready to be harvested, now is the time to incorporate these fresh seasonal items into your recipes and celebrations. Remember to be thankful as the summer starts to wind down and the harvest season begins.

Another old name for this holiday was Loaf-mass. On this day, bread was often shaped into symbols for the late summer such as a Sun or a sheaf of wheat. Today why not bake some whole grain bread and have it with your family dinner? If making bread from scratch sounds too difficult for you, then use a mix and a bread machine. Or how about whipping up a batch of cornbread? Or purchasing a fresh loaf of bread from a local bakery? Once you have your loaf, try this Lughnasadh bread blessing to go with it.

On this day of Lughnasadh, the harvest begins,
Bless us with prosperity, good health, and wisdom.

—Ellen Dugan

5 Saturday
2nd ♐
☽ v/c 3:22 pm
Color: Brown

Celtic Tree Month of Hazel begins

6 Sunday
2nd ♐
☽ enters ♑ 1:19 am
Color: Orange

August

7 Monday

2nd ♑
☽ v/c 9:44 pm
Color: Ivory

Lammas crossquarter day
(Sun reaches 15° Leo)

8 Tuesday

2nd ♑
☽ enters ♒ 3:47 am
Color: Red

*Garnet is associated with self-confidence,
success, and popularity; give the stone
to a friend who has earned a promotion*

☺ Wednesday

2nd ♒
Full Moon 6:54 am
☽ v/c 6:58 pm
Color: Brown

Corn Moon

10 Thursday

3rd ♒
☽ enters ♓ 4:10 am
✴ enters ♍ 9:42 pm
Color: Green

11 Friday

3rd ♓
☿ enters ♌ 12:09 am
Color: Purple

Laurie Cabot withdraws from Salem,
Massachusetts, mayoral race, 1987
Birthday of Edain McCoy, Wiccan author

Set in Eastern Daylight Time (EDT)

Corn Moon

The grains are harvested and being processed inside the sacred threshing house when the joyous Corn Moon beams down upon us. Our celebration of grain—especially as bread—is a primal instinct shared by all human cultures. "Bread is the staff of life," has been so ingrained in our psyches that the first forecast of impending bad weather, such as a hurricane or blizzard, sends us racing to the nearest grocery store to strip it bare of bread products.

We must look to the distant past to understand this bread-buying frenzy through its impact on winter hardship. The latest diet enemy is carbohydrates, but the human body needs parts of all foods to function. Carbohydrates—such as breads—provide energy. Without them we become listless, sleepy; we lose the ability to focus, and to care about things we love. In a time when grain stores could be depleted long before the end of the protein and sodium diet of winter, it must have seemed as if bread was magical, regenerating the spark of life to winter-weary bodies.

—Edain McCoy

---

12 Saturday

3rd ♓
☽ v/c 3:17 am
☽ enters ♈ 4:22 am
♀ enters ♌ 4:21 pm
Color: Gray

---

13 Sunday

3rd ♈
☽ v/c 8:14 pm
Color: Yellow

Aradia de Toscano allegedly
born in Volterra, Italy, 1313
Church of Wicca founded in Australia
by Lady Tamara Von Forslun, 1989

August

14 Monday
3rd ♈
☽ enters ♉ 6:00 am
Color: Silver

*The rowan tree deflects evil energy and
entities from the land where it grows*

○ Tuesday
3rd ♉
☽ v/c 9:51 pm
4th quarter 9:51 pm
Color: Gray

Birthday of Charles Godfrey Leland,
author of *Aradia, Gospel of Witches*, 1824

16 Wednesday
4th ♉
☽ enters ♊ 10:07 am
Color: White

17 Thursday
4th ♊
Color: Purple

Scott Cunningham's first
initiation into Wicca, 1973

18 Friday
4th ♊
☽ v/c 8:30 am
☽ enters ♋ 5:03 pm
Color: Rose

Father Urbain Grandier found
guilty of bewitching nuns at a
convent in Loudoun, France, 1634

19 Saturday
4th ♋
Color: Blue

John Willard and Reverend
George Burroughs put to death
in the Salem Witch trials, 1692

20 Sunday
4th ♋
☽ v/c 3:06 am
Color: Gold

Execution of Lancashire Witches, 1612
Birthday of H. P. Lovecraft, horror
writer and alleged magician, 1890
Birthday of Ann Moura, author and Witch

August

21 Monday

4th ♋
☽ enters ♌ 2:33 am
Color: Lavender

22 Tuesday

4th ♌
Color: Maroon

> Pope John XXII orders the
> Inquisition at Carcassonne to seize
> the property of Witches, sorcerers, and
> those who make wax images, 1320

☽ Wednesday

4th ♌
☽ v/c 2:19 am
☉ enters ♍ 2:22 am
☽ enters ♍ 2:08 pm
New Moon 3:10 pm
Color: Topaz

> Sun enters Virgo

24 Thursday
1st ♍
☿ D 11:20 am
Color: Turquoise

25 Friday
1st ♍
☽ v/c 3:00 pm
Color: Coral

> *Sacred to Athena, the owl*
> *embodies feminine wisdom and intellect*

Silver Footprints

Follow her silver footprints
Up to the highest hill, and
Laugh to see her dancing there:
Luna, round and pregnant with potential.
Merry meet with your people; it's that time
Of month. She'll lead you all
On a quest to find within what you will
Never find without.

—Elizabeth Barrette

26 Saturday
1st ♍
☽ enters ♎ 3:01 am
Color: Indigo

Wearing dark blue protects your emotions
and discourages unwanted personal comments

27 Sunday
1st ♎
☿ enters ♍ 3:30 pm
Color: Amber

August/September

28 Monday
1st ♎
☽ v/c 4:01 am
☽ enters ♏ 3:56 pm
Color: White

*Saffron empowers love spells
and charms of physical desire*

29 Tuesday
1st ♏
Color: Black

Election of Pope Innocent VIII, who issued
bull *Summis Desiderantes Affectibus*, 1484

30 Wednesday
1st ♏
☽ v/c 4:41 pm
Color: Yellow

○ Thursday
1st ♏
☽ enters ♐ 3:00 am
2nd quarter 6:56 pm
Color: Green

Birthday of Raymond Buckland,
who, along with his wife Rosemary,
is generally credited with bringing
Gardnerian Wicca to the United States

1 Friday
2nd ♐
Color: Pink

Set in Eastern Daylight Time (EDT)

2 Saturday

2nd ♐
☽ v/c 3:49 am
☽ enters ♑ 10:34 am
Color: Black

Celtic Tree Month of Vine begins
Birthday of Reverend Paul
Beyerl, Wiccan author

3 Sunday

2nd ♑
Color: Orange

Three initiations of wisdom:
lawful teaching, effective
customs, and instinctive love

September

4 Monday

2nd ♑
☽ v/c 10:24 am
☽ enters ♒ 2:15 pm
♇ D 7:21 pm
Color: Gray

Labor Day

5 Tuesday

2nd ♒
Color: Red

Vetivert breaks hexes and repels thieves

6 Wednesday

2nd ♒
♀ enters ♍ 2:15 am
☽ v/c 5:29 am
☽ enters ♓ 2:56 pm
Color: Topaz

☺ Thursday

2nd ♓
Full Moon 2:42 pm
Color: Turquoise

Harvest Moon
Lunar eclipse 2:52 pm, 15° ♓ 01'

8 Friday

3rd ♓
♂ enters ♎ 12:18 am
☽ v/c 5:02 am
☽ enters ♈ 2:23 pm
Color: Rose

Founding of the Theosophical
Society by H. P. Blavatsky, Henry
Steele Olcott, and others, 1875

Set in Eastern Daylight Time (EDT)

Harvest Moon

The Moon that shines in the September night is called the Harvest or Wine Moon in North America, and its celebration closely resembles many aspects of the Vine Moon of Celtic lore. The Harvest Moon marks the longest reaping period of the year, one that features grapes and other base fruits used in wines. Many European fruits and wines are sacred to deities. Blackberries are sacred to Ireland's Brigid, and in Rome, Bacchus embodies the spirit of Mediterranean wines. In the Middle East, past and present, dark red wines are mixed liberally with natural sugars and consecrated for use as sacraments in religious settings.

Set aside a libation for your patron deity under the Harvest Moon.

Grape and berry, wine and beer,
All hail Bacchus, toast harvest cheer!
With barley blessed beer, and sacred wine rare,
All hail Bacchus and abandon all care!

—Edain McCoy

---

9 Saturday
3rd ♈
Color: Brown

---

10 Sunday
3rd ♈
☽ v/c 4:52 am
☽ enters ♉ 2:30 pm
Color: Amber

Birthday of Carl Llewellyn
Weschcke, owner and president
of Llewellyn Worldwide

September

11 Monday

3rd ♉
Color: Lavender

Birthday of Silver RavenWolf,
Wiccan author

12 Tuesday

3rd ♉
☽ v/c 4:58 pm
☽ enters ♊ 4:59 pm
☿ enters ♎ 5:07 pm
Color: White

Three foundations of wisdom:
discretion in learning, memory in
retaining, and eloquence in telling

13 Wednesday

3rd ♊
Color: Yellow

◖ Thursday

3rd ♊
4th quarter 7:15 am
☽ v/c 12:00 pm
☽ enters ♋ 10:53 pm
Color: Crimson

Phillip IV of France draws up
the order for the arrest of
the French Templars, 1306

Birthday of Henry Cornelius Agrippa,
scholar and magician, 1486

15 Friday

4th ♋
Color: Purple

Onyx increases strength, stability,
and stamina; it's a perfect gift for athletes

Spicy Harvest Soup

2 tbs. butter
2 medium onions, sliced
2 medium carrots, shredded
1 stalk celery, thinly sliced
1 tbs. snipped fresh Italian parsley
2 tsp. freshly grated ginger
2 cloves garlic, minced
½ tsp. ground allspice
4 bouillon cubes
1 cup milk
1 (15 oz.) can pumpkin
8 oz. peeled and deveined
   cooked shrimp

In a covered saucepan, sauté in butter until limp: onions, carrots, celery, parsley, ginger, garlic, and allspice. Stir once or twice. Put mixture in a blender or food processor, add ½ cup of water, and puree. Return to sauce pan and add the bouillon cubes, 2 cups water, milk, and pumpkin. Stir well. When hot, add the shrimp. Serve with a spoonful of sour cream or plain yogurt and some snipped chives. Makes 3 hearty portions.

—K. D. Spitzer

---

16 Saturday

4th ♋
☽ v/c 8:31 pm
Color: Gray

---

17 Sunday

4th ♋
☽ enters ♌ 8:15 am
Color: Gold

Bewitched debuts on ABC-TV, 1964

September

18 Monday
4th ♌
Color: Silver

Abalone shell conveys healing and serenity

19 Tuesday
4th ♌
☽ v/c 8:16 am
☽ enters ♍ 8:07 pm
Color: Black

20 Wednesday
4th ♍
Color: Brown

21 Thursday
4th ♍
Color: Purple

Apple, catnip, mallow, rose, tansy,
valerian, and willow are all feminine herbs

☽ Friday
4th ♍
☽ v/c 7:45 am
New Moon 7:45 am
☽ enters ♎ 9:06 am
Color: White

Solar eclipse 8:07 am, 29° ♍ 20'

Set in Eastern Daylight Time (EDT)

Mabon

As the season of autumn begins, we celebrate the second harvest festival and the Witch's Thanksgiving. The Autumn Equinox marks the time of equal day and night and the beginning of the fall. Meditate on bringing balance into your life this autumn. Get outside and rejoice in the changing leaves and the glorious colors, scents, and textures of the fall.

Traditional harvest themes work into your magical decorations beautifully. Try arranging apples or ornamental corn in a basket or group cute miniature pumpkins and gourds together on your shelf or mantle. Add some pretty pinecones and autumn leaves in their rich colors and dress things up a bit. Tie a rustling bundle of cornstalks to your front porch to celebrate the earth's blessings at harvest-tide. Hang up a trio of ornamental corn on your front door. Bless it in the name of the Triple Goddess for protection and prosperity.

> *Three ears of corn for the Maiden, Mother, and Crone,*
> *Protect well our house, and bring prosperity home.*

—Ellen Dugan

---

23 Saturday

1st ♎
☉ enters ♎ 12:03 am
Color: Blue

Rosh Hashanah
Mabon/Fall Equinox
Sun enters Libra

---

24 Sunday

1st ♎
☽ v/c 10:11 am
☽ enters ♏ 9:54 pm
Color: Yellow

Ramadan begins

September/October

25 Monday
1st ♏
Color: White

Senate passes an amendment (705)
attached by Senator Jesse Helms to House
Resolution 3036 (1986 budget bill),
denying tax-exempt status to any organization
that espouses satanism or witchcraft, 1985

26 Tuesday
1st ♏
Color: Maroon

Joan Wiliford hanged at Faversham,
England, 1645; she testified that
the Devil came to her in the form of a
black dog that she called "Bunnie"

27 Wednesday
1st ♏
☽ v/c 1:32 am
☽ enters ♐ 9:16 am
Color: Topaz

28 Thursday
1st ♐
Color: Green

*Wear apple green when you need to
face challenges; it energizes you
and helps you see new opportunities*

29 Friday
1st ♐
☽ v/c 4:45 pm
☽ enters ♑ 6:01 pm
Color: Coral

Set in Eastern Daylight Time (EDT)

Between the Worlds

As green leaves turn gold and
Umber, Kore goes underground.
Tall winds whisper aging wisdom.
Until now, all has been preparation.
Matron of the Dead, she stands
Numinous between the worlds.

— Elizabeth Barrette

☽ Saturday

1st ♑
♀ enters ♎ 6:02 am
2nd quarter 7:04 am
Color: Indigo

Celtic Tree Month of Ivy begins

---

1 Sunday

2nd ♑
☽ v/c 11:16 pm
☽ enters ♒ 11:24 pm
Color: Orange

Birthday of Isaac Bonewitz,
Druid, magician, and Witch

Birthday of Annie Besant,
Theosophical Society president, 1847

October

2 Monday

2nd ≈
☿ enters ♏ 12:38 am
♃ D 10:02 pm
Color: Gray

Yom Kippur
Birthday of Timothy Roderick,
Wiccan author

3 Tuesday

2nd ≈
☽ v/c 4:14 pm
Color: White

4 Wednesday

2nd ≈
☽ enters ♓ 1:33 am
⚷ enters ♎ 7:57 pm
Color: Yellow

President Reagan signs JR 165 making
1983 "The Year of the Bible" (public law
#9728Q); the law states that the Bible is
the word of God and urges a return to
"traditional" Christian values, 1982

5 Thursday

2nd ♓
☽ v/c 4:33 pm
Color: Turquoise

Three things which the good poet preserves:
memory of the praiseworthy, delight in
thought, instruction in knowledge

☺ Friday

2nd ♓
☽ enters ♈ 1:32 am
Full Moon 11:13 pm
Color: Pink

Blood Moon

Set in Eastern Daylight Time (EDT)

Blood Moon

The name Blood Moon comes from the act of slaughtering animals for winter food, and from the reddish cast often seen shadowing the Moon on cool October nights. In Celtic traditions this is the Ivy Moon, and one of its correspondences is binding magic. They are perfect complements to one another at this season, when we are compelled to bind the blood of the sovereign Lord to the land he rules.

Even in the festive circle of October's esbat we are aware that the solar year is marking the death of our God, and we put ourselves into the care of the wise, but icy, crone Goddess. The Goddess, who is the land, will soon be in her virgin aspect once more, and must bestow sovereignty over the land to the most fit and able man.

> *Blessed crone of our dark, cold nights,*
> *Give us your moonglow as our guiding light;*
> *His blood into earth, your earth into womb,*
> *Waiting for Yuletide to break open his tomb.*

—Edain McCoy

---

7 Saturday

3rd ♈
☽ v/c 4:05 pm
Color: Brown

Sukkot begins
Birthday of Arnold Crowther, stage
magician and Gardnerian Witch, 1909

---

8 Sunday

3rd ♈
☽ enters ♉ 1:04 am
Color: Gold

October

9 Monday

3rd ♉
☽ v/c 1:07 pm
Color: Lavender

Columbus Day (observed)

10 Tuesday

3rd ♉
☽ enters ♊ 2:06 am
Color: Red

If autumn leaves blow into
the house, they bring good luck

11 Wednesday

3rd ♊
☽ v/c 8:22 pm
Color: Brown

12 Thursday

3rd ♊
☽ enters ♋ 6:21 am
☿ D 5:11 pm
Color: Green

Birthday of Aleister Crowley, 1875

◑ Friday

3rd ♋
4th quarter 8:25 pm
Color: White

Sukkot ends
Jacques de Molay and other
French Templars arrested by
order of King Phillip IV, 1306

Set in Eastern Daylight Time (EDT)

14 Saturday

4th ♋
☽ v/c 2:27 am
☽ enters ♌ 2:38 pm
Color: Gray

*Allspice, borage, clove, dill, garlic, hops,
linden, mandrake, peppermint, rue,
and woodruff are all masculine herbs*

15 Sunday

4th ♌
Color: Amber

October

16 Monday

4th ♌

☽ v/c 5:00 pm

Color: White

Yarrow can banish evil influences
from a person, a place, or an object

17 Tuesday

4th ♌

☽ enters ♍ 2:15 am

Color: Black

18 Wednesday

4th ♍

Color: Topaz

Birthday of Nicholas Culpepper,
astrologer and herbalist, 1616

19 Thursday

4th ♍

☽ v/c 4:18 am

☽ enters ♎ 3:19 pm

Color: Purple

20 Friday

4th ♎

Color: Rose

Birthday of Selena Fox, Circle Sanctuary

Set in Eastern Daylight Time (EDT)

Fried "Samhain Toads"

1 egg
1 cup milk
2 tbs. molasses
2 tbs. honey
1 cup flour
¼ tsp. salt
¼ tsp. baking soda
2 tsp. baking powder
1 cup stone-ground cornmeal

Beat the egg; add milk, molasses, and honey. Blend dry ingredients; stir into egg mixture. Batter should be soft, but firm enough to stay on spoon. In a deep pot, heat cooking oil to 375°F. Using a soup spoon, gather up a dollop of batter and, using another spoon to push it off, drop it carefully into hot fat. It will expand into outlandish forms when it hits the hot oil. Only cook a few at a time until golden. To make apple cider syrup, pour a quart of fresh apple cider into a pan that is wider than it is tall. Bring cider to a boil; let it simmer until it is a thickened but still runny syrup (makes 1½ cups).

—K. D. Spitzer

21 Saturday
4th ♎
✳ enters ♎ 9:16 pm
Color: Blue

Blue spinel is a soothing stone that brings peace and transcendence

☽ Sunday
4th ♎
New Moon 1:14 am
☽ v/c 1:57 am
☽ enters ♏ 3:54 am
Color: Yellow

October

23 Monday

1st ♏
☉ enters ♏ 9:26 am
♂ enters ♏ 12:38 pm
Color: Silver

Sun enters Scorpio

24 Tuesday

1st ♏
☽ v/c 2:56 am
♀ enters ♏ 5:57 am
☽ enters ♐ 2:53 pm
Color: Gray

Ramadan ends

25 Wednesday

1st ♐
Color: White

Jacques de Molay first interrogated
after Templar arrest, 1306

26 Thursday

1st ♐
☽ v/c 2:02 pm
☽ enters ♑ 11:47 pm
Color: Crimson

De Molay and thirty-one other Templars
confess to heresy in front of an assembly of
clergy; all later recant their confessions, 1306
Sybil Leek dies of cancer, 1982

27 Friday

1st ♑
Color: Coral

Circle Sanctuary founded, 1974

Set in Eastern Daylight Time (EDT)

Edge of Night

To catch the edge of night,
Walking between Sun and shadow,
Is to find the place where reality
Leaves off and magic begins.
In a time that is not a time,
Go softly, go slowly, and
Hope to catch a glimpse of
That which lies beyond.

—Elizabeth Barrette

---

28 Saturday
1st ♑
☿ ℞ 3:16 pm
☽ v/c 9:30 pm
Color: Indigo

Celtic Tree Month of Reed begins

☽ Sunday
1st ♑
♆ D 2:56 am
☽ enters ♒ 5:17 am
2nd quarter 4:25 pm
Color: Orange

Daylight Saving Time ends at 2 am
MacGregor Mathers issues manifesto
calling himself supreme leader of
the Golden Dawn; all members had to sign an
oath of fealty to him, 1896
Birthday of Frater Zarathustra, who founded
the Temple of Truth in 1972

October/November

30 Monday
2nd ≈
Color: Ivory

House-Senate conferees drop the Senate
provision barring the IRS from granting
tax-exempt status to groups that promote
satanism or witchcraft, 1985

PACT (Pagan Awareness Coalition for Teens)
established in Omaha, Nebraska, 2001

31 Tuesday
2nd ≈
☽ v/c 12:31 am
☽ enters ♓ 9:10 am
Color: Maroon

Samhain/Halloween
Martin Luther nails his ninety-five theses
to the door of Wittenburg Castle Church,
igniting the Protestant revolution, 1517

Covenant of the Goddess founded, 1975

1 Wednesday
2nd ♓
Color: Yellow

All Saints' Day
Aquarian Tabernacle Church established
in the United States, 1979

2 Thursday
2nd ♓
☽ v/c 2:54 am
☽ enters ♈ 10:46 am
Color: Green

Circle Sanctuary purchases land
for nature preserve, 1983

3 Friday
2nd ♈
Color: White

Set in Eastern Standard Time (EST)

Samhain

The black cat is a classic Samhain/Halloween symbol. The cat has been linked to witchcraft, magic, and the Goddess for centuries. For example, the Egyptian cat goddess Bast was typically portrayed as a black cat. Later, the Romans identified Bast with Diana, who was called the "Queen of the Witches" during the Middle Ages. Historically, little distinction has been made between Witches, faeries, goddesses, and the feline, for during different periods in history the cat was believed to represent them all in physical form.

This Samhain, why not work a little cat magic for protection and good luck in the Celtic New Year with your feline friend? Hold your cat in your lap, light a white candle, and repeat the charm three times.

> *This Samhain night I call Diana, goddess of the Moon,*
> *I cast for protection and good luck with this Witchy tune.*
> *My feline friend and I do work this spell as one,*
> *As we will so mote it be, an' let it harm none.*

—Ellen Dugan

---

4 Saturday

2nd ♈
☽ v/c 3:04 am
☽ enters ♉ 11:05 am
Color: Brown

The cinquefoil, a flowerlike emblem of five petals, represents Aphrodite and her sacred roses

---

☺ Sunday

2nd ♉
Full Moon 7:58 am
Color: Gold

Mourning Moon

November

6 Monday

3rd ♉
☽ v/c 5:17 am
☽ enters ♊ 11:46 am
Color: Lavender

7 Tuesday

3rd ♊
Color: Red

Election Day (general)
Samhain crossquarter day
(Sun reaches 15° Scorpio)

8 Wednesday

3rd ♊
☽ v/c 6:15 am
☽ enters ♋ 2:46 pm
Color: Brown

Sentencing of Witches in
Basque Zugarramurdi trial, 1610
Marriage of Patricia and Arnold Crowther
officiated by Gerald Gardner, 1960

9 Thursday

3rd ♋
Color: White

Patricia and Arnold Crowther
married in civil ceremony, 1960

10 Friday

3rd ♋
☽ v/c 3:58 pm
☽ enters ♌ 9:34 pm
Color: Pink

The goldfinch represents fruitfulness and gallantry

Set in Eastern Standard Time (EST)

Mourning Moon

The harvest is over and food provisions are readied for winter. Homes are patched against the cold winds to come—winds foreshadowed by the nights of heavy frost. Under this Moon of the slowing season, we mourn with our Goddess for the death of our God.

As the Mourning Moon reaches fullness we must remember our mourning always ends. Our crone is also the mother of the new God, who will be born to her in less than six weeks time.

> Crying crone, the banshee wail,
> An ancient myth does tells your tale;
> Your consort slain shall be reborn,
> From you, his mother, on Yuletide's morn.
> Virgin, mother, crone of cold,
> The three in one are triads old;
> Grant us your wisdom, unveil and show,
> That life goes on even under the snow.

—Edain McCoy

---

11 Saturday

3rd ♌
Color: Gray

Veterans Day

☽ Sunday

3rd ♌
4th quarter 12:45 pm
Color: Yellow

November

13 Monday
4th ♌
☽ v/c 3:29 am
☽ enters ♍ 8:18 am
Color: Silver

14 Tuesday
4th ♍
Color: Black

Turquoise teaches the wearer to be more empathic

15 Wednesday
4th ♍
☽ v/c 5:41 pm
☽ enters ♎ 9:14 pm
Color: White

Aquarian Tabernacle Church
established in Canada, 1993

16 Thursday
4th ♎
Color: Turquoise

17 Friday
4th ♎
♀ enters ♐ 3:02 am
☿ D 7:25 pm
Color: Rose

Birthday of Israel Regardie, occultist
and member of the OTO, 1907

18 Saturday

4th ♎
☽ v/c 12:41 am
☽ enters ♏ 9:46 am
Color: Blue

Aleister Crowley initiated into the
Golden Dawn as Frater Perdurabo, 1898

19 Sunday

4th ♏
Color: Orange

Birthday of Theodore
Parker Mills, Wiccan elder, 1924

☽ Monday

4th ♏
♅ D 1:09 am
New Moon 5:18 pm
☽ v/c 6:54 pm
☽ enters ♐ 8:15 pm
Color: Ivory

Church of All Worlds
incorporates in Australia, 1992

21 Tuesday

1st ♐
Color: Maroon

22 Wednesday

1st ♐
☉ enters ♐ 6:02 am
☽ v/c 8:19 pm
Color: Topaz

Sun enters Sagittarius

23 Thursday

1st ♐
☽ enters ♑ 4:25 am
♃ enters ♐ 11:43 pm
Color: Purple

Thanksgiving Day
Birthday of Lady Tamara Von Forslun,
founder of the Church of Wicca and the
Aquarian Tabernacle Church in Australia

24 Friday

1st ♑
☽ v/c 8:43 pm
Color: Coral

The Holly King's Favorite

1 (12 oz.) package fresh cranberries
1 orange
1 fifth good vodka
1½ cups granulated sugar

Coarsely chop cranberries. Zest the orange into strips with a veggie peeler, making sure there's no white pith. Combine the cranberries, orange parings, and vodka in a glass jar. Cover and store in a dark place for four weeks, shaking occasionally. Strain.

Make a simple syrup by combining sugar and ¾ cup water and bringing to a boil for one minute. Cool and stir into cranberry-orange vodka. Add more simple syrup if desired, and toss in a 2-inch cinnamon stick if desired. Let sit two to four weeks before serving. Package in smaller containers with ribbons and labels for gift giving. Delicious when added to cranberry relish or a Tequila Sunrise or a Cape Cod.

—K. D. Spitzer

25 Saturday
1st ♑
☽ enters ♒ 10:41 am
Color: Indigo

Celtic Tree Month of Elder begins
Dr. John Dee notes Edward
Kelly's death in his diary, 1595

26 Sunday
1st ♒
Color: Amber

Solar herbs include bay, cinnamon,
marigold, rosemary, and tormentil

27 Monday
1st ♒
☽ v/c 8:00 am
☽ enters ♓ 3:20 pm
Color: Gray

*Wear honeysuckle oil to enhance
your power and communication*

○ Tuesday
1st ♓
2nd quarter 1:29 am
Color: Black

29 Wednesday
2nd ♓
☽ v/c 11:29 am
☽ enters ♈ 6:30 pm
Color: Yellow

30 Thursday
2nd ♈
Color: Crimson

Birthday of Oberon Zell,
Church of All Worlds
Father Urbain Grandier imprisoned in
France for bewitching nuns, 1633

1 Friday
2nd ♈
☽ v/c 1:41 pm
☽ enters ♉ 8:26 pm
Color: White

Birthday of Anodea Judith,
president, Church of All Worlds

Taproots

With a toothless smile
And a nod, she goes when
No one is looking.
Is this old woman
Nothing but a
Ghost of her former glory?
Make yourself still, quiet.
Only then will you hear
On the floor her tapping cane.
No one knows more than she.
                    —Elizabeth Barrette

---

2 Saturday
2nd ♉
Color: Brown

*Nephrite, a relative of jade, has similar
powers of health and prosperity but costs less*

---

3 Sunday
2nd ♉
☽ v/c 7:31 pm
☽ enters ♊ 10:05 pm
Color: Orange

December

☺ Monday
2nd ♊
♅ enters ♏ 7:31 am
Full Moon 7:25 pm
Color: Lavender

Long Nights Moon

5 Tuesday
3rd ♊
☽ v/c 6:12 pm
♄ ℞ 11:06 pm
♂ enters ♐ 11:58 pm
Color: Black

Pope Innocent VIII reverses the
Canon Episcopi by issuing the bull
Summis Desiderantes Affectibus, removing
obstacles to Inquisitors, 1484
Death of Aleister Crowley, 1947

6 Wednesday
3rd ♊
☽ enters ♋ 1:00 am
☽ v/c 8:13 pm
Color: White

Death of Jacob Sprenger, coauthor
of the *Malleus Maleficarum*, 1495
Birthday of Dion Fortune, member
of the Golden Dawn, 1890

7 Thursday
3rd ♋
Color: Green

8 Friday
3rd ♋
☿ enters ♐ 12:51 am
☽ enters ♌ 6:52 am
Color: Pink

*The hummingbird represents joy
and harmony; it can be a divine
messenger or a guide for lost souls*

Long Nights Moon

The name "Long Nights Moon" stirs up images of the Winter Solstice—a date that has been designated for spiritual observance for more than twelve thousand years.

Beneath the Long Nights Moon, light a candle of white or silver to honor the lunar deities. Thank them for the light of the night sky and the knowledge of the sunlight's return in the months to come. Let the candle burn itself out when you are finished.

Lady Luna, queen of the long night,
Grant me safety until the sunlight;
Your silver orb a comfort gives,
We know in you our God still lives.
Lord of moonlight, no less than your queen,
We await the moment when the Earth grows green;
Sleep in the womb of your mother most fair,
Who sleeps in the Earth until we waken her there.

—Edain McCoy

---

9 Saturday

3rd ♌
Color: Black

---

10 Sunday

3rd ♌
☽ v/c 3:35 pm
☽ enters ♍ 4:31 pm
Color: Yellow

December

11 Monday
3rd ♍
♀ enters ♑ 12:33 am
Color: White

○ Tuesday
3rd ♍
4th quarter 9:32 am
☽ v/c 9:32 pm
Color: Red

The blue jay is a trickster;
seeing one foretells a change

13 Wednesday
4th ♍
☽ enters ♎ 5:00 am
Color: Topaz

First papal bull against black magic
issued by Alexander IV, 1258

14 Thursday
4th ♎
Color: Turquoise

15 Friday
4th ♎
☽ v/c 10:33 am
☽ enters ♏ 5:42 pm
Color: Rose

Sugilite is a rich purple stone that
helps dispel negative emotions and habits

Set in Eastern Standard Time (EST)

Snowdreams

Within the sleeping earth
Infinite seeds dream of rain.
Now snow cloaks the land,
Terrible in its power and wonder.
Even the Sun bows before it, awaiting
Rebirth at solstice time.
>   —Elizabeth Barrette

---

16 Saturday
4th ♏
Color: Indigo

Hanukkah begins

---

17 Sunday
4th ♏
☽ v/c 6:31 pm
Color: Gold

December

18 Monday
4th ♏
☽ enters ✗ 4:10 am
Color: Silver

19 Tuesday
4th ✗
Color: Gray

Spices associated with Mars include
cumin, ginger, pepper, and pimento

☽ Wednesday
4th ✗
☽ v/c 9:01 am
New Moon 9:01 am
☽ enters ♑ 11:39 am
Color: Yellow

21 Thursday
1st ♑
☽ v/c 11:05 am
☉ enters ♑ 7:22 pm
Color: White

Yule/Winter Solstice
Sun enters Capricorn

22 Friday
1st ♑
☽ enters ♒ 4:49 pm
Color: Purple

Janet and Stewart Farrar begin
their first coven together, 1970

Set in Eastern Standard Time (EST)

Yule

On the day of the Winter Solstice, celebrate the birth of the Sun God in simple ways. Tuck fresh sprigs of berried holly around the house for protection and good luck. (Make sure the berries are well out of reach if you have small children.) Drape some pine roping over your doorways to ward your home and to encourage good health and joy. Rumor has it that by doing this you are inviting the faeries of winter into your home so they can  have a warm place to celebrate the Yuletide festivities. Look for Yule-themed ornaments in the shapes of golden Suns and stars, sparkly snow-flakes, and crystal icicles, and work in a metallic star garland to add some enchantment to your Yule tree. As you go to "deck the halls," try this charm to bless your home during this festive time of the year.

When a Witch decks the halls with boughs of holly,
Expect that the Yuletide feast will be jolly.
Now add a touch of magic and a pinch of glee,
Welcome renewal in Yuletide's season of peace.

—Ellen Dugan

---

23 Saturday

1st ≈
Color: Blue

Hanukkah ends

---

24 Sunday

1st ≈
☽ v/c 3:09 pm
☽ enters ♓ 8:43 pm
Color: Amber

Christmas Eve
Celtic Tree Month of Birch begins

December

25 Monday
1st ♓
Color: Ivory

Christmas Day

Feast of Frau Holle, Germanic weather goddess who was believed to travel through the world to watch people's deeds; she blessed the good and punished the bad

26 Tuesday
1st ♓
☽ v/c 10:05 pm
Color: Maroon

Kwanzaa begins

Dr. Fian arraigned for twenty counts of witchcraft and treason, 1590

☾ Wednesday
1st ♓
☽ enters ♈ 12:04 am
♀ enters ♒ 6:47 am
2nd quarter 9:48 am
☿ enters ♑ 3:54 pm
Color: Brown

Birthday of Gerina Dunwich, Wiccan author

28 Thursday
2nd ♈
♃ enters ♓ 7:54 pm
☽ v/c 9:54 pm
Color: Purple

29 Friday
2nd ♈
☽ enters ♉ 3:08 am
Color: Coral

Hematite promotes focus;
wear it when you need to concentrate

Set in Eastern Standard Time (EST)

30 Saturday
2nd ♉
☽ v/c 9:37 pm
Color: Indigo

31 Sunday
2nd ♉
☽ enters ♊ 6:16 am
Color: Orange

New Year's Eve
Castle of Countess Bathory of Hungary
raided, 1610; accused of practicing black
magic, she murdered scores of the local
townsfolk; she was walled up in a room in
her castle, where she later died

About the Authors

ELIZABETH BARRETTE serves as the managing editor of *PanGaia* and the assistant editor of *SageWoman*. She has been involved with the Pagan community for more than sixteen years, and has done much networking with Pagans in her area, including coffeehouse meetings and open sabbats. Her other writing fields include speculative fiction and gender studies. She lives in central Illinois and enjoys herbal landscaping and gardening for wildlife.

DALLAS JENNIFER COBB lives an enchanted life in a waterfront village and writes about what she loves most: mothering, gardening, magic, and alternative economics. She is forever scheming novel ways to pay the bills, when she is not running on country roads or wandering the beach with her daughter. Her essays have appeared in *Three-Ring Circus* and *Far From Home*—recent anthologies from Seal Press. This year her video documentary was produced on TV Ontario's *Planet Parent*. She is a regular contributor to Llewellyn's almanacs.

ELLEN DUGAN, the "Garden Witch," is a psychic-clairvoyant and has been a practicing Witch for over eighteen years. Ellen is a master gardener and teaches classes on flower folklore and gardening at a community college. She is the author of the Llewellyn books *Garden Witchery*, *Elements of Witchcraft: Natural Magick for Teens*, and *Seven Days of Magick*. Ellen and her family live in Missouri.

RAVEN GRIMASSI, a teacher and practitioner of the Craft for over thirty years, is the author of several Llewellyn titles: *Wiccan Mysteries*, *Encyclope-*

dia of Wicca & Witchcraft, Wiccan Magick, The Witches' Craft, The Witch's Familiar, Spirit of the Witch, Italian Witchcraft, and *Hereditary Witchcraft*.

JENNIFER HEWITSON has been a freelance illustrator since 1985. Her illustrations have appeared in various local and national newspapers and magazines, including the *Wall Street Journal*, the *Washington Post*, the *Los Angeles Times, US News & World Report*, and *Ladybug* magazine. She also works for advertising and packaging clients such as Disney and the San Diego Zoo. Jennifer has created a line of greeting cards for Sun Rise Publications, and has also illustrated several children's books. Her work has been recognized and awarded by numerous organizations, including *Communication Arts* magazine, *Print* magazine, Society of Illustrators Los Angeles, and *How* magazine.

JAMES KAMBOS holds a degree in history and geography. He has had a lifelong interest in folk magic traditions and has authored numerous articles on this subject. When not writing and painting from his home in the beautiful Appalachian hills of Ohio, he celebrates the changing seasons working in his herb and flower garden.

EDAIN MCCOY has been in the Craft since 1981 and has been researching alternative spiritualities since her teens. Areas of special interest are Celtic, Appalachian, Curanderismo, Eclectic Wicca, Jewitchery, and Irish Witta. She is listed in the reference guides *Contemporary Authors, Who's Who Among American Women*, and *Who's Who In America*. Articles written by her have appeared in *FATE, Circle, Enlightenments*, and similar periodicals.

DANNY PHARR is an author and master firewalk instructor. He founded Wings of Fire Seminars with the mission to provide individuals with a safe environment to discover joy, encourage personal achievement and growth, and engage in life-changing experiences. His first book, *The Moon and Everyday Living*, was published in 2000.

K. D. SPITZER has been a solitary practitioner for more than twenty years. She is an experienced astrologer, teacher, and writer who uses astrological magic in her spell working. She is the publisher and editor of *The Country Wisdom Almanac*, an uncomplicated compendium designed to bring the power of the planets to daily life.

ABBY WILLOWROOT is the founder and director of the Goddess 2000 Project, the Spiral Goddess Grove, and Willowroot Real Magic Wands. Since 1965 Abby has been a full-time professional Goddess artist, wand maker, and writer. Nine pieces of Ms. Willowroot's jewelry are in the Smithsonian Institution's permanent collection. Her work has appeared in many metaphysical publications.

Daily Magical Influences

Each day is ruled by a planet with specific magical influences.

Monday (Moon): peace, healing, caring, psychic awareness

Tuesday (Mars): passion, courage, aggression, protection

Wednesday (Mercury): study, travel, divination, wisdom

Thursday (Jupiter): expansion, money, prosperity, generosity

Friday (Venus): love, friendship, reconciliation, beauty

Saturday (Saturn): longevity, endings, homes

Sunday (Sun): healing, spirituality, success, strength, protection

Color Correspondences

Colors are associated with each day, according to planetary influence.

Monday: gray, lavender, white, silver, ivory

Tuesday: red, white, black, gray, maroon, scarlet

Wednesday: yellow, brown, white, topaz

Thursday: green, turquoise, white, purple, crimson

Friday: white, pink, rose, purple, coral

Saturday: brown, gray, blue, indigo, black

Sunday: yellow, orange, gold, amber

Lunar Phases

Waxing, from New Moon to Full Moon, is the ideal time to do magic to draw things to you.

Waning, from Full Moon to New Moon, is a time for study, meditation, and magical work designed to banish harmful energies.

The Moon's Sign

The Moon continuously moves through each sign of the zodiac, from Aries to Pisces, staying about two-and-a-half days in each sign. The Moon influences the sign it inhabits, creating different energies that affect our day-to-day lives.

Aries: Good for starting things. Things occur rapidly, but quickly pass. People tend to be argumentative and assertive.

Taurus: Things begun now last longest, tend to increase in value, and become hard to change. Brings out an appreciation for beauty and sensory experience.

Gemini: Things begun now are easily changed by outside influence. Time for shortcuts, communication, games, and fun.

Cancer: Stimulates emotional rapport between people. Supports growth and nurturing. Tend to domestic concerns.

Leo: Draws emphasis to the self, to central ideas or institutions, away from connections with others and emotional needs.

Virgo: Favors accomplishment of details and commands from higher up. Focus on health, hygiene, and daily schedules.

Libra: Favors cooperation, compromise, social activities, balance, friendship, and partnership.

Scorpio: Increases awareness of psychic power. Precipitates psychic crises and ends connections thoroughly. People tend to brood and become secretive.

Sagittarius: Encourages confidence and flights of imagination. This is an adventurous, philosophical, and athletic Moon sign. Favors expansion and growth.

Capricorn: Develops strong structure. Focus on traditions, responsibilities, and obligations. A good time to set boundaries and rules.

Aquarius: Rebellious energy. Time to break habits and make abrupt change. Personal freedom and individuality is the focus.

Pisces: The focus is on dreaming, nostalgia, intuition, and psychic impressions. A good time for spiritual or philanthropic activities.

2006 Eclipses

March 14, 6:49 pm; Lunar eclipse 24° ♍ 15'
March 29, 5:33 am; Solar eclipse 8° ♈ 35'
September 7, 2:52 pm; Lunar eclipse 15° ♓ 01'
September 22, 8:07 am; Solar eclipse 29° ♍ 20'

2006 Full Moons

Cold Moon: January 14, 4:48 am
Quickening Moon: February 12, 11:44 pm
Storm Moon: March 14, 6:35 pm
Wind Moon: April 13, 12:40 pm
Flower Moon: May 13, 2:51 am
Strong Sun Moon: June 11, 2:03 pm
Blessing Moon: July 10, 11:02 pm
Corn Moon: August 9, 6:54 am
Harvest Moon: September 7, 2:42 pm
Blood Moon: October 6, 11:13 pm
Mourning Moon: November 5, 7:58 am
Long Nights Moon: December 4, 7:25 pm

Planetary Retrogrades in 2006

Saturn	℞	11/22/05	4:01 am	— Direct	04/05/06	8:54 am
Venus	℞	12/24/05	4:36 am	— Direct	02/03/06	4:18 am
Mercury	℞	03/02/06	3:29 pm	— Direct	03/25/06	8:42 am
Jupiter	℞	03/04/06	1:02 pm	— Direct	07/06/06	3:19 am
Pluto	℞	03/29/06	7:40 am	— Direct	09/04/06	7:21 pm
Neptune	℞	05/22/06	9:05 am	— Direct	10/29/06	2:56 am
Uranus	℞	06/19/06	3:40 am	— Direct	11/20/06	1:09 am
Mercury	℞	07/04/06	3:33 pm	— Direct	07/28/06	8:39 pm
Mercury	℞	10/28/06	3:16 pm	— Direct	11/17/06	7:25 pm
Saturn	℞	12/05/06	11:06 pm	— Direct	04/19/07	5:24 pm

Set in Eastern Time. All times corrected for Daylight Saving Time.

Moon Void-of-Course Data for 2006

JANUARY

Last Aspect Date	Time	New Sign Sign	New Time
12/31	4:09 am	1 ≈	7:14 am
3	6:44 am	3 ♓	7:43 am
5	7:10 am	5 ♈	9:44 am
7	9:34 am	7 ♉	2:09 pm
9	1:56 pm	9 ♊	8:58 pm
11	8:46 pm	12 ♋	5:50 am
14	4:48 am	14 ♌	4:31 pm
16	7:35 pm	17 ♍	4:49 am
19	5:12 pm	19 ♎	5:49 pm
22	3:53 am	22 ♏	5:28 am
23	4:53 pm	24 ♐	1:38 pm
26	10:24 am	26 ♑	5:31 pm
28	2:57 am	28 ≈	6:09 pm
30	11:00 am	30 ♓	5:32 pm

FEBRUARY

Last Aspect Date	Time	New Sign Sign	New Time
1	11:06 am	1 ♈	5:46 pm
3	1:33 pm	3 ♉	8:31 pm
5	4:00 pm	6 ♊	2:32 am
8	10:04 am	8 ♋	11:33 am
10	3:53 pm	10 ♌	10:44 pm
13	6:48 am	13 ♍	11:13 am
15	10:21 pm	16 ♎	12:09 am
18	11:59 am	18 ♏	12:11 pm
20	5:02 am	20 ♐	9:38 pm
22	9:06 pm	23 ♑	3:16 am
24	7:58 pm	25 ≈	5:14 am
26	11:25 pm	27 ♓	4:56 am
28	11:14 pm	3/1 ♈	4:18 am

MARCH

Last Aspect Date	Time	New Sign Sign	New Time
2/28	11:14 pm	1 ♈	4:18 am
3	2:42 am	3 ♉	5:22 am
5	3:14 am	5 ♊	9:37 am
7	11:09 am	7 ♋	5:38 pm
9	3:41 pm	10 ♌	4:42 am
12	10:38 am	12 ♍	5:23 pm
14	11:33 pm	15 ♎	6:12 am
17	11:31 am	17 ♏	5:59 pm
20	2:54 am	20 ♐	3:43 am
22	4:47 pm	22 ♑	10:36 am
23	6:30 pm	24 ≈	2:21 pm
26	10:18 am	26 ♓	3:33 pm
28	10:20 am	28 ♈	3:31 pm
30	10:41 am	30 ♉	4:00 pm

APRIL

Last Aspect Date	Time	New Sign Sign	New Time
1	10:52 am	1 ♊	6:49 pm
3	10:24 pm	4 ♋	2:15 am
5	1:19 pm	6 ♌	12:25 pm
8	7:02 pm	9 ♍	12:58 am
11	10:59 am	11 ♎	1:46 pm
13	6:42 pm	14 ♏	1:08 am
15	2:29 pm	16 ♐	10:19 am
18	2:41 pm	18 ♑	5:13 pm
19	9:15 pm	20 ≈	9:56 pm
22	7:03 pm	23 ♓	12:43 am
24	8:35 pm	25 ♈	2:12 am
26	9:44 pm	27 ♉	3:27 am
28	9:31 pm	29 ♊	5:58 am

MAY

Last Aspect Date	Time	New Sign Sign	New Time
1	7:13 am	1 ♋	11:17 am
3	2:35 pm	3 ♌	8:18 pm
6	1:01 am	6 ♍	8:20 am
8	1:49 pm	8 ♎	9:10 pm
11	1:15 am	11 ♏	8:24 am
13	2:51 am	13 ♐	4:56 pm
15	4:15 pm	15 ♑	10:59 pm
17	10:10 am	18 ≈	3:19 am
20	5:20 am	20 ♓	6:39 am
22	2:45 am	22 ♈	9:24 am
24	5:16 am	24 ♉	12:00 am
26	6:39 am	26 ♊	3:19 pm
28	7:23 pm	28 ♋	8:33 pm
31	12:42 am	31 ♌	4:51 am

JUNE

Last Aspect Date	Time	New Sign Sign	New Time
2	1:34 pm	2 ♍	4:17 pm
4	8:30 pm	5 ♎	5:08 am
7	8:15 am	7 ♏	4:41 pm
9	6:10 am	10 ♐	1:05 am
11	10:34 pm	12 ♑	6:19 am
13	12:50 pm	14 ≈	9:32 am
16	4:44 am	16 ♓	12:05 pm
18	10:08 am	18 ♈	2:54 pm
20	5:20 pm	20 ♉	6:23 pm
22	8:44 pm	22 ♊	10:49 pm
24	8:02 pm	25 ♋	4:48 am
27	12:02 pm	27 ♌	1:09 pm
29	2:24 pm	30 ♍	12:15 am

JULY

Last Aspect Date	Time	New Sign Sign	New Time
2	2:58 am	2 ♎	1:06 pm
4	3:17 pm	5 ♏	1:13 am
6	3:54 pm	7 ♐	10:13 am
9	6:31 am	9 ♑	3:25 pm
11	4:58 pm	11 ≈	5:46 pm
13	10:23 am	13 ♓	6:59 pm
15	3:56 pm	15 ♈	8:39 pm
17	9:33 pm	17 ♉	11:44 pm
20	1:48 am	20 ♊	4:38 am
22	11:17 am	22 ♋	11:28 am
24	5:07 am	24 ♌	8:24 pm
26	8:32 pm	27 ♍	7:36 am
29	9:05 am	29 ♎	8:27 pm
31	9:54 pm	8/1 ♏	9:08 am

AUGUST

Last Aspect Date	Time	New Sign Sign	New Time
7/31	9:54 pm	1 ♏	9:08 am
3	5:08 am	3 ♐	7:13 pm
5	3:22 pm	6 ♑	1:19 am
7	9:44 pm	8 ≈	3:47 am
9	6:58 pm	10 ♓	4:10 am
12	3:17 am	12 ♈	4:22 am
13	8:14 pm	14 ♉	6:00 am
15	9:51 pm	16 ♊	10:07 am
18	8:30 am	18 ♋	5:03 pm
20	3:06 am	21 ♌	2:33 am
23	2:19 am	23 ♍	2:08 pm
25	3:00 pm	26 ♎	3:01 am
28	4:01 am	28 ♏	3:56 pm
30	4:41 pm	31 ♐	3:00 am

SEPTEMBER

Last Aspect Date	Time	New Sign Sign	New Time
2	3:49 am	2 ♑	10:34 am
4	10:24 am	4 ≈	2:15 pm
6	5:29 am	6 ♓	2:56 pm
8	5:02 am	8 ♈	2:23 pm
10	4:52 am	10 ♉	2:30 pm
12	4:58 pm	12 ♊	4:59 pm
14	12:00 pm	14 ♋	10:53 pm
16	8:31 pm	17 ♌	8:15 am
19	8:16 am	19 ♍	8:07 pm
22	7:45 am	22 ♎	9:06 am
24	10:11 am	24 ♏	9:54 pm
27	1:32 am	27 ♐	9:16 am
29	4:45 pm	29 ♑	6:01 pm

OCTOBER

Last Aspect Date	Time	New Sign Sign	New Time
1	11:16 pm	1 ≈	11:24 pm
3	4:14 pm	4 ♓	1:33 am
5	4:33 pm	6 ♈	1:32 am
7	4:05 pm	8 ♉	1:04 am
9	1:07 pm	10 ♊	2:06 am
11	8:22 pm	12 ♋	6:21 am
14	2:27 am	14 ♌	2:38 pm
16	5:00 pm	17 ♍	2:15 am
19	4:18 am	19 ♎	3:19 pm
22	1:57 am	22 ♏	3:54 am
24	2:56 am	24 ♐	2:53 pm
26	2:02 pm	26 ♑	11:47 pm
28	9:30 pm	29 ≈	5:17 am
31	12:31 am	31 ♓	9:10 am

NOVEMBER

Last Aspect Date	Time	New Sign Sign	New Time
2	2:54 am	2 ♈	10:46 am
4	3:04 am	4 ♉	11:05 am
6	5:17 am	6 ♊	11:46 am
8	6:15 am	8 ♋	2:46 pm
10	3:58 pm	10 ♌	9:34 pm
13	3:29 am	13 ♍	8:18 am
15	5:41 pm	15 ♎	9:14 pm
18	12:41 am	18 ♏	9:46 am
20	6:54 pm	20 ♐	8:15 pm
22	8:19 pm	23 ♑	4:25 am
24	8:43 pm	25 ≈	10:41 am
27	8:00 am	27 ♓	3:20 pm
29	11:29 am	29 ♈	6:30 pm

DECEMBER

Last Aspect Date	Time	New Sign Sign	New Time
1	1:41 pm	1 ♉	8:26 pm
3	7:31 pm	3 ♊	10:05 pm
5	6:12 pm	6 ♋	1:00 am
6	8:13 pm	8 ♌	6:52 am
10	3:35 pm	10 ♍	4:31 pm
12	9:32 pm	13 ♎	5:00 am
15	10:33 am	15 ♏	5:42 pm
17	6:31 pm	18 ♐	4:10 am
20	9:01 am	20 ♑	11:39 am
21	11:05 am	22 ≈	4:49 pm
24	3:09 pm	24 ♓	8:43 pm
26	10:05 pm	27 ♈	12:04 am
28	9:54 pm	29 ♉	3:08 am
30	9:37 pm	31 ♊	6:16 am

Set in Eastern Time. All times corrected for Daylight Saving Time.

Name:

Address, City, State, Zip:

Home Phone: Office Phone:

E-mail: Birthday:

Name:

Address, City, State, Zip:

Home Phone: Office Phone:

E-mail: Birthday:

Name:

Address, City, State, Zip:

Home Phone: Office Phone:

E-mail: Birthday:

Name:

Address, City, State, Zip:

Home Phone: Office Phone:

E-mail: Birthday:

Name:

Address, City, State, Zip:

Home Phone: Office Phone:

E-mail: Birthday:

Name:

Address, City, State, Zip:

Home Phone: Office Phone:

E-mail: Birthday:

Name:

Address, City, State, Zip:

Home Phone: Office Phone:

E-mail: Birthday:

Name:

Address, City, State, Zip:

Home Phone: Office Phone:

E-mail: Birthday:

Name:

Address, City, State, Zip:

Home Phone: Office Phone:

E-mail: Birthday:

Name:

Address, City, State, Zip:

Home Phone: Office Phone:

E-mail: Birthday:

Name:

Address, City, State, Zip:

Home Phone: Office Phone:

E-mail: Birthday:

Name:

Address, City, State, Zip:

Home Phone: Office Phone:

E-mail: Birthday:

Name:

Address, City, State, Zip:

Home Phone: Office Phone:

E-mail: Birthday:

Name:

Address, City, State, Zip:

Home Phone: Office Phone:

E-mail: Birthday:

Name:

Address, City, State, Zip:

Home Phone: Office Phone:

E-mail: Birthday:

Name:

Address, City, State, Zip:

Home Phone: Office Phone:

E-mail: Birthday:

Name:

Address, City, State, Zip:

Home Phone: Office Phone:

E-mail: Birthday:

Name:

Address, City, State, Zip:

Home Phone: Office Phone:

E-mail: Birthday:

Name:

Address, City, State, Zip:

Home Phone: Office Phone:

E-mail: Birthday:

Name:

Address, City, State, Zip:

Home Phone: Office Phone:

E-mail: Birthday:

Name:

Address, City, State, Zip:

Home Phone: Office Phone:

E-mail: Birthday:

Name:

Address, City, State, Zip:

Home Phone: Office Phone:

E-mail: Birthday:

Name:

Address, City, State, Zip:

Home Phone: Office Phone:

E-mail: Birthday:

Name:

Address, City, State, Zip:

Home Phone: Office Phone:

E-mail: Birthday:

Name:

Address, City, State, Zip:

Home Phone: Office Phone:

E-mail: Birthday:

Name:

Address, City, State, Zip:

Home Phone: Office Phone:

E-mail: Birthday:

Name:

Address, City, State, Zip:

Home Phone: Office Phone:

E-mail: Birthday:

Name:

Address, City, State, Zip:

Home Phone: Office Phone:

E-mail: Birthday:

Name:

Address, City, State, Zip:

Home Phone: Office Phone:

E-mail: Birthday:

Name:

Address, City, State, Zip:

Home Phone: Office Phone:

E-mail: Birthday: